Developing Skill

A Guide to 3v3 Soccer Coaching

Peter Prickett

DARK
RIVER

Published in 2018 by Dark River, an imprint of Bennion Kearny Limited.

Copyright © Dark River

Peter Prickett has asserted his right under the Copyright Designs and Patents Act 1988 to be identified as the author of this work

ISBN: 978-1-911121-54-1

Published by Dark River, an imprint of Bennion Kearny Limited
6 Woodside
Churnet View Road
Oakamoor
ST10 3AE

Many thanks to Garth Smith for his fantastic cover design.

Table of Contents

Chapter 6 – Pitch Types | 103

Chapter 7 – A Practical Conclusion | 125

1

A Starting Point

What do we love about football?

This question is short and simple but has myriad possible answers.

There are core and key overall aspects. Competition, glory, drama, storytelling, teamwork, artistry, and skill. As fans, there are two things that we want, victory and entertainment. Sometimes, one without the other is not enough. Teams can achieve genuine (or relative) success yet have an unhappy fan base because they have not witnessed a style of football that thrills them.

The greatest players are those who provide entertainment and excitement. It may manifest in different ways, but it is near universal that onlookers will be enraptured by moments of high quality. The higher the quality they see, the higher the entertainment levels. This then produces moments that last forever and keep fans glued to the sport.

Football is filled with contradictions. One of these is that a great team needs great individuals from whom great quality derives. Every link in the chain needs to be strong, while some individuals may emerge to be stronger than others. Between 2008 and 2018, the world has been enthralled by the collective play of Barcelona. Their wonderful tiki-taka style of pass and move football often requires no more than one or two touches, yet each of those touches needs to be a work of craftsmanship. Such a high quality of team play is only possible because of the outstanding quality of each player.

Barcelona have had one other thrilling aspect to their football. Although managers might have come and gone, one player has been constant through this period – Lionel Messi. At Barcelona, he has been the ultimate individual within the team. The player with such pure quality that fast passing is no problem, and neither is dribbling past two or three players. Nor striking spectacularly from long-range or drawing in several opponents before releasing the perfect pass. We love the team, but we also love the individual.

Messi and Barcelona are not the only great individual and team to grace the game of football. During this period, there has been the fascinating duel between Messi and Ronaldo, sparking the never-ending debate about who is better. Or who is the greatest? Is either of these players superior to the legends of the past? Pele, Maradona, Cruyff, Di Stéfano, or any others people choose to bring into the conversation. Each of these players had the quality, skill, decision making, and imagination to execute consistently and – most importantly perhaps – during the big moments. This ultimately is what coaches want for each of their young players. Can we somehow create the environment and practices that will give players the opportunity to develop top-level attributes?

It is grossly unrealistic to expect every young player to develop in this way, but unless we give them the chance, we will never know if they can. As coaches, we have limited time with our players, and that will always be an obstacle. More than that, no matter how much time we actually do have, we will always wish for more. The required abilities of a top level player form a very lengthy list.

Technical	Tactical	Physical	Psychological	Social
Receiving skills	Adapt to the game	Agility, balance, and coordination	Confidence	Behaviour
Turning skills	Exploit strengths and weaknesses	Speed/speed endurance	Creativity	Reflection
Travelling with the ball	Apply individual, unit, and team responsibilities	Flexibility	Concentration	Teamwork
Passing over varied distances	Adopt different playing styles and formations	Power	Communication	Relationships
Attacking and defending skills	Perform effectively against different styles and formations	Strength	Control	Accountability
Finishing skills	Deal with varied environmental conditions	Resilience	Commitment	Responsibility
Aerial ability		Recovery		Independence

(From the England DNA)

This many areas are daunting and need distilling. Time is going to dictate how much effect a coach can have on these areas. Sessions per week, and minutes per session, increase incrementally as young players and coaches move up the stages from grassroots to academy. In the main, coaches at all levels will be able to most affect technical, tactical and psychological outcomes at any level.

To my mind, the key to hitting such heights is what a player is capable of with the ball. The ball and the player need to form a deeply satisfying long-term relationship. One in which the player has full command of everything that the ball does. The player should be able to demand that the ball momentarily appears to defy physics and behave in a manner unexpected to their opponent. Immense amounts of practice are required, and many coaches assign time during training to this, but it takes more. Huge numbers of hours spent between a child and a ball are needed to perfect, refine, and experiment, in a quest to find their preferred moves.

It all starts with the ability to dribble. A 'dribble first' mindset will pay big dividends in the long term. Players need to see an opponent and feel confident that they can take that player on. If they have been brought up as a passer, they will only ever pass when they see an opponent, eventually panicking when one comes too close. When a dribbler sees pressure (and an opponent), the mindset is different. This is not to panic; this is opportunity. When they get older, it is easier to teach a player who dribbles too much to pass than it is to teach a passer to become a dribbler.

The great dribblers are the players who best fulfil what we love about football. These players represent the footballer we are in our dreams. The ability to deceive and outmanoeuvre their opponent with shifts of the ball, jinks of the body, and astounding balance. Such entertainers are not the reserve of trophy-laden teams only. Such exciting dribblers can bring joy to teams with average results. In the Premier League alone, we have seen Juninho, Ginola, and Kinkladze bewitch with their ball playing ability, even though their teams did not achieve great results. A lack of any 'end product' is often levelled at football's dribblers but their tricks and skills are a device to create space and openings; once those are created, they are then judged on the shot, pass, or cross. What is often forgotten is that teams need players to have the ability to create those openings in the first place!

To get here, we need 1v1. If we are going to master the ball, we need to practise it against an opponent to achieve our dribbling mindset. If we work on ball mastery, and always move straight into situations where it will not be used, then an opportunity is wasted. 1v1s may occur in games where we have overloaded attacking situations, but fast passing outcomes are far more likely. Playing 1v1, there is no escaping it – players need to dribble. Players need to face up to, and face off against, other players. Both as attackers and defenders. Defending against your immediate opponent is just as important as attacking. If a player cannot defend one on one, they will be picked out. They will be the link in the chain that opponents exploit. It will no longer be 5v5 or 11v11; the game will be 4v5 or 10v11. Not all evenly numbered match ups are equal.

Chapter 1

1v1 setups need to be varied in order to replicate the conditions of the game. Not all one on one situations in a game will be face to face. Some will be with an opponent immediately behind, some will have the opponent coming in from the side, some will be against a goalkeeper rather than against a defender. This variation will increase the number of decisions a player needs to make, and the constraints they need to deal with. Should they accelerate off their first touch to escape through a gate in front of them? Do they twist and turn until they can get the defender off balance and can escape through a side gate? Or can they shift the ball enough to create the opportunity to shoot? The decisions affecting the attacker will also affect the defender; we will sometimes put the defender in a situation that does not favour them, but the opposite can also be true.

For a book about 3v3, this is a lot of discussion about 1v1 being vital to the game. If 1v1 is so important, why don't we focus on that? Because there is one key decision missing from 1v1. The decision to pass. The absence of this possibility removes a number of actions from the dribbler's arsenal. As well as simply being able to pass, the player is unable to fake to pass. If there are no teammates to pass to, why would a defender believe the action to fake pass? Similarly, if the set up does not involve goals, why would the defender buy a fake shot? We want the player to focus on how to take on an opponent, but the realism eventually needs to come in.

The logical progression is into 2v2 and usually onto 4v4 and 5v5.

Which is what I used to do. I even designed numerous practices for this. After a few weeks working on 2v2s, I felt there were certain problems. The 2v2 situations were just not dynamic enough. The game was mostly played in a flat line. Sometimes in an offset line. There was very little opportunity to make effective runs off the ball, and simple man-to-man defending worked the majority of the time. An extra player was required to create a more dynamic and realistic environment.

Any child will tell you that with three players a triangle can easily be created. When it comes to passing the football, a triangle is the optimal shape (arguably a diamond is, depending on whether a coach sees a diamond as a diamond or as two triangles). The player on the ball has two options, immediately creating more possible movements for attackers and more challenging situations for defenders. An element of choosing a formation can be introduced simply by moving the points of the triangle. Should a team defend with two points closest to their goal or with one? What difference does that make to the opposition? It is the same position for attackers. Do we push two players high and wide or push just one up high acting as a centre-forward? These choices will then affect the actions of the game. In one case, we might see more up, back, and through actions. In another, more overlaps could be possible. The set up now gives attacking players lines to break through with a dribble or pass that did not previously exist in a 2v2.

These advantages over 2v2 are also true of 4v4 and 5v5. My experiences have shown that even in 4v4s and 5v5s, certain young players do not get a significant number of touches of the ball. By playing 3v3, players will receive more touches than in 4v4 and 5v5 but fewer than 1v1 and 2v2. However, they will be able to achieve a greater number of technical and tactical decisions than within the 1v1 and 2v2 environments. Within a 3v3 game, those 1v1 and 2v2 situations will occur with regularity. Not only that, there will be 1v0 situations where a player receives the ball under no pressure. There will be 2v1 attacking overloads, 1v2 defending overloads, 3v1 attacking overloads, 1v3 defending overloads, 3v2 attacking overloads and 2v3 defending overloads. There will be a greater number of opportunities to dribble but also decisions on whether to pass, shoot, or dribble. This is football. The game is fluid and rarely is it genuinely 11v11. The immediate actions of the game usually take place within a small space. If a photo was taken and cropped, the actions in that space would look a lot like a small sided game. By playing 3v3, we are helping to prepare players for the variable small moments of the larger game.

On a practical level, I have found it easier to plan for 3v3-based sessions than for 4v4 or 5v5. The general guideline is for 16 players per coach. That is a maximum which would provide two 4v4 games. It is a maximum though, not a minimum. Many coaches of young players will not have squads of that size. I have found it easier to plan for 2x3v3 and scale up, changing one 3v3 into a 4v4 or just adding a player to make 3v3+1 (magic man/joker), than to make 4v4 practices and scale down.

As coaches, we are always looking for ways to get the most out of the time that we spend with our players. We want players to have the capability to take people on and win games on their own but at the same time to be able to combine and attack with fluency. They also have to be able to defend, to drop off, and pick the right moment to go in and pressure hard. If players are capable on the ball, this all becomes easier. Give them the most touches you can while still creating football-based decisions.

Using the setup described in this book, I hope to help create an environment in which players can become masters of the ball and masters of decision making. Where players can develop a great tactical understanding while developing their technical ability. Players who can play with freedom but also make choices based on ingrained knowledge of the game that they are playing. Can we develop the modern footballer using the 3v3 principles while still allowing them to play?

I believe we can.

2
Warming Up

People can tie themselves in knots when it comes to the warm-up. The warm-up before the session, and the warm-up before the game, are different propositions. Before the game, it is most important to find a routine. Something that is consistent and which triggers the process in players' minds that they are about to play a match. The older the players are, the more important this becomes. With young players, there is no problem warming up for a game by playing a game.

Debates rage about the importance of a 'physical' warm-up. Young players are very unlikely to pull muscles. For them, getting into a game groove is the priority before a game. This will generally mean lots of touches, movement, and finding game speed. Older players are likely to need some form of dynamic stretching and movement but they also have to get enough touches and game-based actions to ready themselves for competition.

At a session, this changes, although – once again – there is no problem in starting off with a match for children. Kids do not warm-up before they play a game during lunch break. I am yet to see a school kid pull a muscle at break time.

The game may be a beginning for the session, or another type of exercise may suit the needs of a certain set of players. From the game, there will need to be a transition into the main body of the session. The problem that often faces coaches is just how to get started. Which element to focus on during the warm-up, and how much space the warm-up takes up. If a warm-up space needs to be cleared before the main session can begin, this can eat into precious time and cause confusion.

The square is a simple set up that requires only four cones and anything from one to five balls. Variations can accommodate two to five players (though it is possible for one player to perform dribbling moves or keep-ups in the square while waiting for others to arrive). The players can organise this themselves when they arrive at training and add their own twist to the exercises.

From a minimal setup, a session can be pushed towards whatever topic the coach desires. Time can be spent developing the technical base of the players or moving straight into more competitive situations. If the players become familiar with the setup, they can choose their activity and take ownership of their own development. All from an initial four cones.

Square 1 – Criss Cross

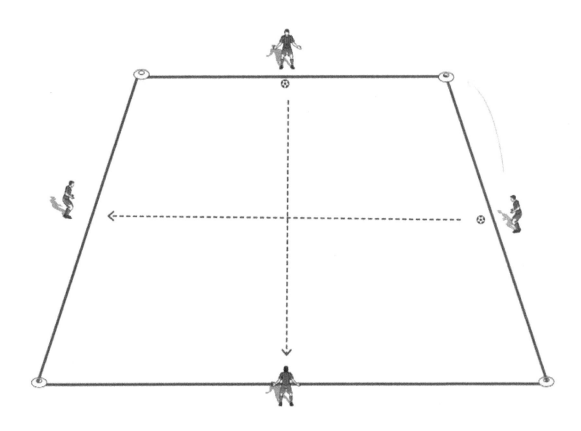

1. Pass across.
2. Move to touch the cone to your left after passing, return to the centre, receive the pass, pass again then touch the cone to the right. Return to the centre and repeat.
3. Check away from the middle to receive the pass at the corner, return to the middle after passing. Alternate corners.
4. From the centre, take a first touch towards the cone before passing. (First touch with inside foot, outside foot, sole, chop, etc.).
5. Control the ball with one foot and pass with the other.
6. Roll with the sole from one foot to the other before passing.

Square 2 – Lofted Passes

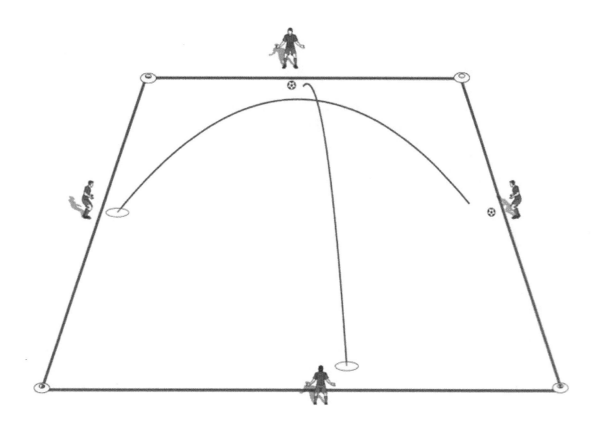

1. Throw the ball across to your teammate to control (chest, thigh, instep, etc.).
2. Chip/scoop the ball to your partner to control.
3. Create a pass where it is all performed in one movement (scoop, flick pass, drag lace pass).
4. Headers across the square.
5. Headers around the square, keeping the ball up.
6. Header wars – Treat your line as a goal to protect. Throw the ball up in the air to try to head past your partner, or head their attempt straight back at goal.

Square 3 – Over Under

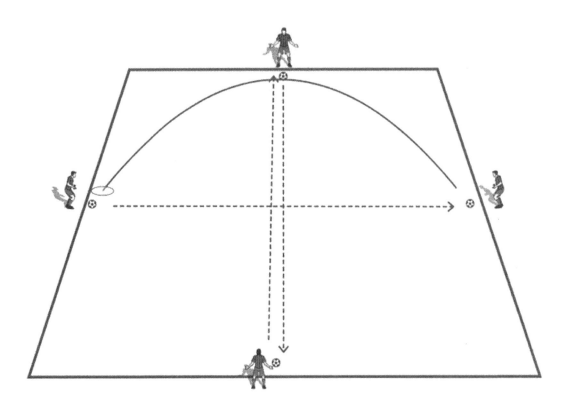

1. Both players, in their pair, have a ball. They pass on the ground to each other at the same time.
2. Both players have a ball. One passes low, the other scoops the ball over that pass.
3. Both players have a ball. One passes low, the other flicks the ball up and volleys it over the low pass.

Square 4 – Dribbling

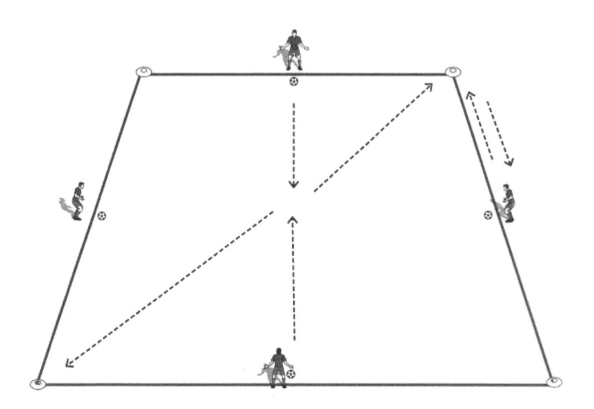

1. Mirror, mirror. Copy your partner's dribbling moves as you both dribble from side to side.
2. Dribble towards the right-hand cone. Perform a turning move or change of direction move (chop, drag back, foot roll, etc.) to return to the centre. Then dribble out to the left-hand cone and turn.
3. While dribbling out to the side cones, perform toe taps (or an alternative movement) before dribbling to the next cone.
4. All four players dribble towards the centre of the square at the same time. Break away to the right-hand cone. Perform a move as you break away (step over, 360, drag push, etc.)
5. When all four players meet in the middle turn right (inside cuts, outside cuts, etc.). Ensure this is also done to the left.

Square 5 – Synchronisation

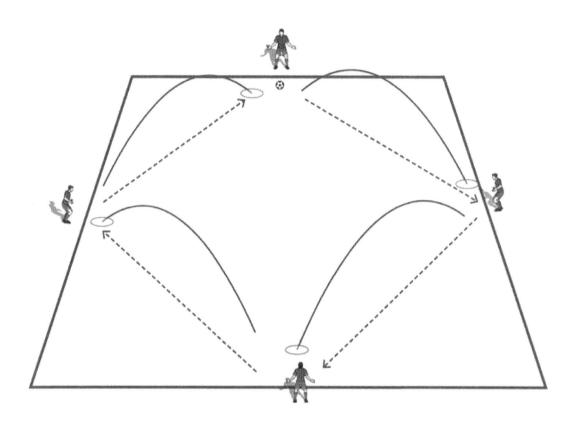

1. One ball is being kept up around the square. Increase the number of balls being kept up as the players improve.
2. One ball is passed around the square from left to right. This should be passed two-touch to practice the action of opening out the body. Try to switch the ball from one foot to the other for faster passes. Increase the number of footballs to challenge synchronisation.
3. As above but chipping/scooping the ball around the square.
4. Switch direction on the coach's call/signal. The players could give the signal or call themselves.

Square 6 – Face Off

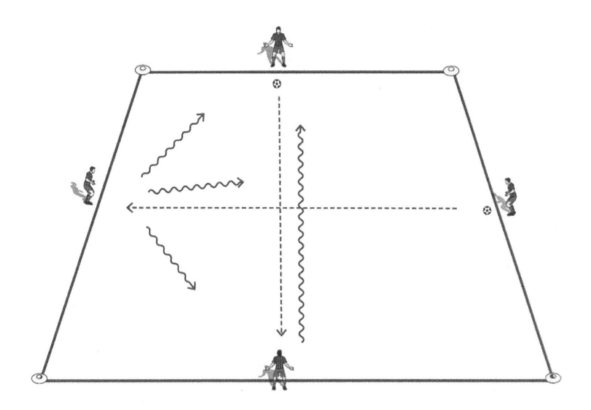

1. One versus one. One pair passes across the square to their partner. In the other pair, one player dribbles across the square and scores a point if they get past their opponent and over the line. If the defender wins the ball, attack the opponent's line for a point.
2. One versus three. The player with the ball can escape out of the square past any of the three opponents. Start with the player in the middle.
3. One versus three tag. All players have a ball. The nominated player goes into the middle and can escape through any side, including the one they just vacated. Outside players must dribble with the ball to block the escape. They may tag the player as he tries to escape.

Square 7 – Knock It Down

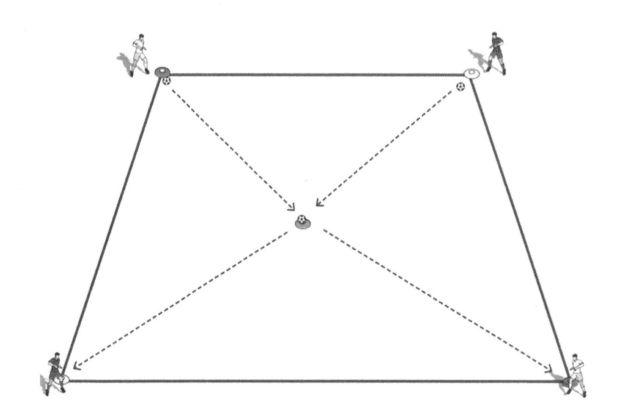

1. Knock the ball off the cone in the middle with a pass. Two players (e.g. white shirts) work together as a team. The two striped players also work as a team. Each team has their own ball. Score a point each time the ball is knocked off the cone. First to x number of points wins.
2. Chip the ball over the ball on the cone. Score a point each time the ball clears the ball on the cone and reaches your partner.

Square 8 – Combinations 1

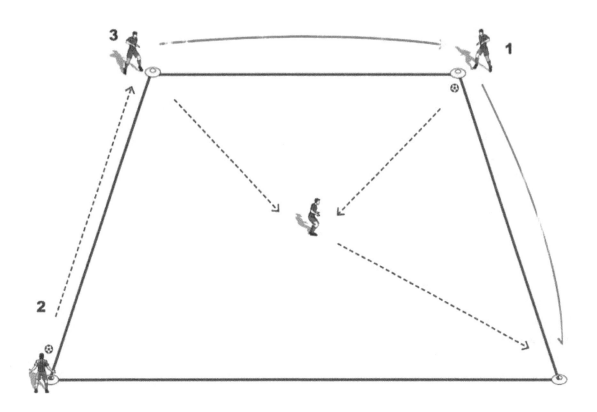

A midfielder passing exercise. The central player needs to check his/her shoulders and observe the movement around him.

a) Player 1 passes to the middle player. They play a 1-2 and player 1 arrives with the ball at the next cone.

b) Player 2 passes to player 3 who then plays a 1-2 with the middle player and arrives at the next cone.

c) Player 1 passes to player 2 who then plays a 1-2 with the middle player and arrives at the next cone.

The exercise continues in a cycle before the middle player is swapped.

Square 9 – Combinations 2

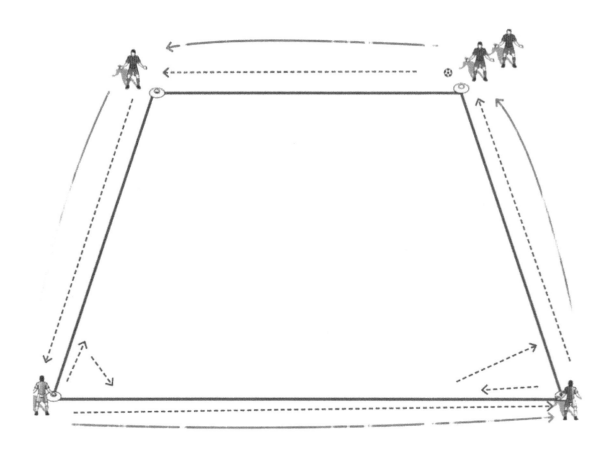

1. Five players. Pass the ball, follow. Pass along the floor. One or two touch play. Encourage players to make double movements away from the cone before receiving.
2. Play a 1-2 before setting the ball to the next passer.
3. Play the longer of the passes in the air.
4. Following the 1-2 pass, the ball must go diagonally across the area in an 'up back and through' style.

Square 10 – Rotation

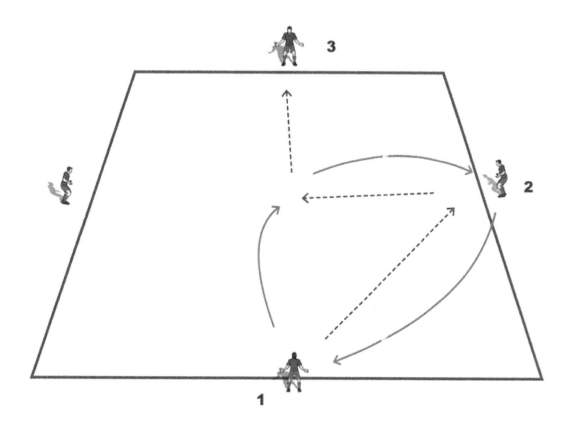

1. Simple rotation. 1 passes to 2. 2 sets back inside for 1 who passes to 3. 2 takes the position of 1. 1 takes the position of 2. Repeat in the opposite direction.
2. Play one touch.
3. Play with the ball in the air.

Square 11 – Long Passes

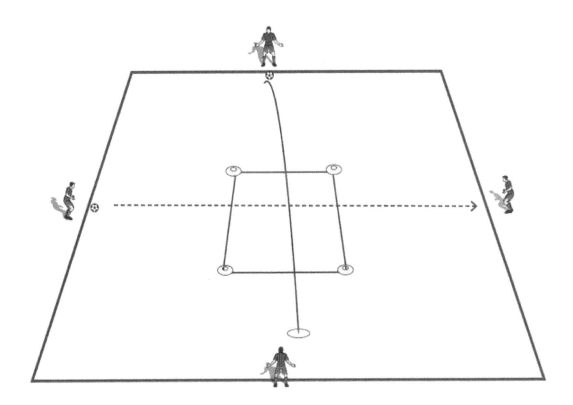

1. Long distance passing. The ball needs to travel through the square on the way to your partner.
2. The ball needs to clear the square before reaching your partner.
3. Your partner runs into the square to receive the ball, then passes it back (coordinate between the pairs, run backwards out of the square).
4. One ball only. Run into the square and then lay off first time to either of the two players who did not play the ball in. If the pass is lofted, this lay off could be a volley or header.

Square 12 – Mini Rondo

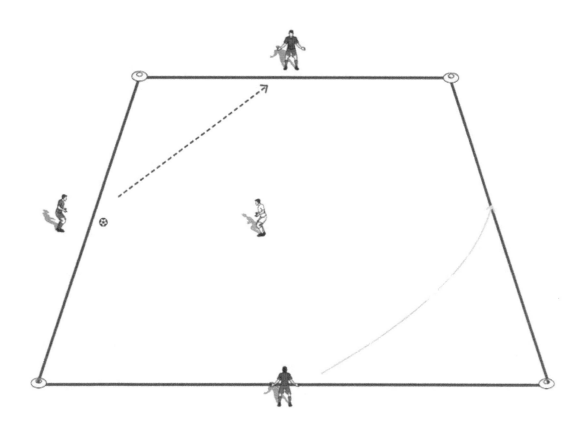

1. Simple rondo. Movement to fill the empty side and keep the ball away from the player in the middle.
2. If there are five players, fill each side and play one touch.

3
1v1

The beginning of everything.

Repetition is generally ill-advised unless it is required to push on a key point. In this case, I must repeat myself because (to my mind) everything begins with one specific thought process.

Dribbling is a mindset. It is a mindset that is learned early on in a player's football life. The shouts from coaches and parents to "pass", "shoot", or "get rid" all discourage the dribbler. The calls erode the mindset… often before it has even begun to form.

It is easier to teach a dribbler to pass when they get older than it is to teach a passer to dribble when they are older.

If a young player always looks to pass after they receive the ball, their response to seeing pressure from an opponent will be to try to give the ball to someone else. If a young player always looks to dribble after they receive the ball, they will respond to pressure from an opponent by attempting to go past that opponent. Or opponents, plural. Although this chapter is about one versus one, in the reality of the game there will be situations where a dribbler is one versus two, three, four or five players – particularly if the opposition are in a deep defensive set up. When teams "park the bus", exceptional dribblers hold the key to unlocking the defence and breaking through the lines.

If a player does not have the mindset that an opponent is something to relish (rather than someone to fear) they will not be able to dribble. The idea of potential reward for beating an opponent should far outweigh the possible risks of losing possession. Much of that comes from the environment that the player develops in. Are they told to pass all the time? Is the play always one and two touch? Are children criticised and labelled for being greedy ball hogs? Or are they encouraged to express themselves – to show their abilities and be free to experiment on the pitch? After all, it is only a game of children's football.

The benefits to having multiple players who are comfortable one versus one (or against greater odds) really start to show when the players begin to mature. If every player is competent defending one on one, a team will be able to defend with solidity. If a number of players on a team are excellent when taking on defenders that is when real advantages are created. In June 2017, France defeated England in a friendly at the Stade de France, 3-2. France had a player sent off but were still able to attack very effectively. The reason for this was that they had Ousmane Dembélé, Kylian Mbappé, Thomas Lemar and Paul Pogba; all players with wonderful dribbling ability. Not all one versus ones are equal. When the attacker is superior to the defender, a one versus one becomes an attacking overload. France effectively had four overloads despite being a player down.

How many overloads can a team create? If France started the game with four exceptional one versus one players, they were effectively playing 15v11. What if a team has six exceptional players? Are we playing 17v11? Where does this stop? In a way, it stops before it even begins because there is only one ball. Football is not 11v11 for the player on the ball, it is likely to be 1v1, 1v2, 1v3, 2v1, 3v1, 2v2 and so forth because the ball is only really being affected by what is happening in the close vicinity. The effect of being superior – one against one – is less that of an overload and more that of an elimination. With each player, the dribbler passes their influence on, and the immediate action of the game is taken away. Turning a 1v3 into a 1v2 into a 1v1 and into 1v0. This is particularly useful when we have players who are capable of dribbling from deep positions and breaking through defensive lines. Gerard Piqué, Franz Beckenbauer, and Alan Hansen were fantastic at taking the ball from their defensive zones past the opposition forwards, then the midfielders, and encroaching on the opposition defence, creating not only chances but panic. Midfielders and forwards who can outplay their immediate foe are highly prized and end up with legendary status, especially in our multimedia world where flashes of skill are preserved forever.

Children adore these moments. They are inspired by these moments, and they want to replicate these moments. Dribbling is about more than being effective with the ball. Being able to manipulate the ball at will is a wonderful boost to the self-esteem of young footballers. Being that little bit closer to their heroes and having the ability to produce the same skill or trick that the greatest player in the world does is an enormous boost. When they can constantly replicate that move in match situations, an entirely new level is reached. One where confidence, competence, self-esteem, and effectiveness are all heightened.

To help children get their moves match-ready, we need to give them one versus one situations within their sessions. Ball mastery and technical exercises are fantastic, but we need to apply full pressure at some point. That pressure is not just face to face but comes from behind and from the side as well. If we can ensure that then our young players are being given the opportunity, they can become one versus one masters, with and without the ball.

1 – Columns

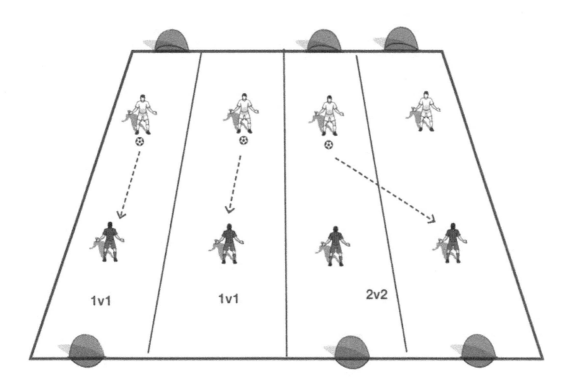

1v1   1v1   2v2

1. The first player passes across to their partner who attacks them, looking to create enough space to score in the mini goal. If the defender wins the ball, they can score in their opponent's mini goal.
2. Alternatively, the player with the ball has the target of crossing the defender's end line or stopping the ball on the line.
3. Progress to 2v2 to introduce basic combination play and more convincing feints. The defenders also have the opportunity to practice communication.

2 – Quick Turns

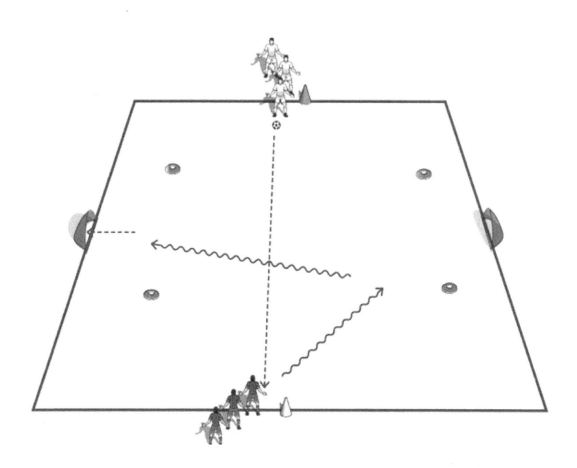

1. The defender passes the ball across to the attacker to start the practice. The attacker can gates close to the mini goal. If the defender wins the ball, they score in either of the mini goals. Encourage twisting and turning combined with sharp acceleration.

Alternatives

- No gates. Encourage a good first touch and fast, accurate finishing.
- No mini goals. Move the cones into the position of the goals. Players score a point by passing through the gates.

3 – Beating an Opponent - Face to Face

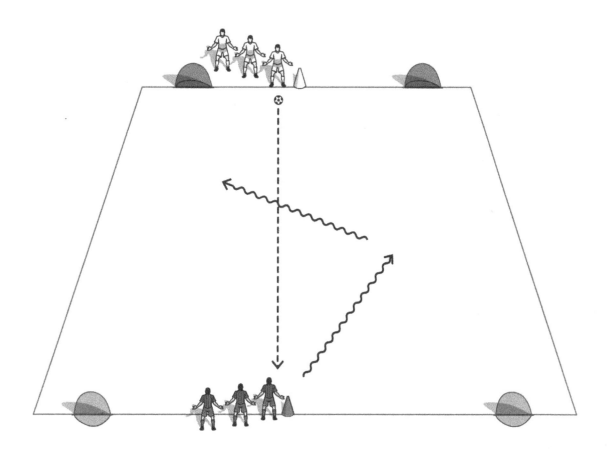

1. White passes to stripe. Stripe tries to score in either of the mini goals at the white team's end. If white win the ball, they can attack the mini goals at stripe's end. This practice is face to face; encourage fake shots and change of direction moves with fast acceleration. Do the attackers have to go past the defender to score or do they just need to create enough space to shoot?
2. If the attacker loses the ball, the next player in the line can step in to represent a covering defender. Should that player win the ball, launch a 2v1 attack.

4 – Beating an Opponent - Diagonal

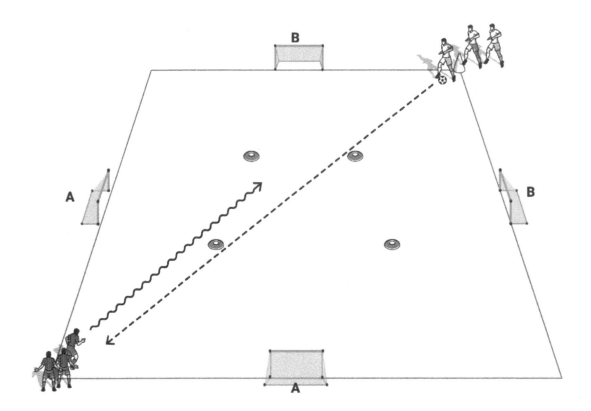

1. White passes across to stripe. Stripe can score in either of the goals marked B once they have entered or passed through the central square. If white wins the ball, they can score in either of the goals marked A. Work on developing an accurate long pass, good first touch, acceleration, and sharp change of direction.
2. Remove the central square and add goalkeepers in front of each goal (two from each team). These can also act as passing options, creating a 3v3.
3. Play 2v2 with the square still in.
4. Play 2v2 with goalkeepers.

5 – Facing Multiple Opponents

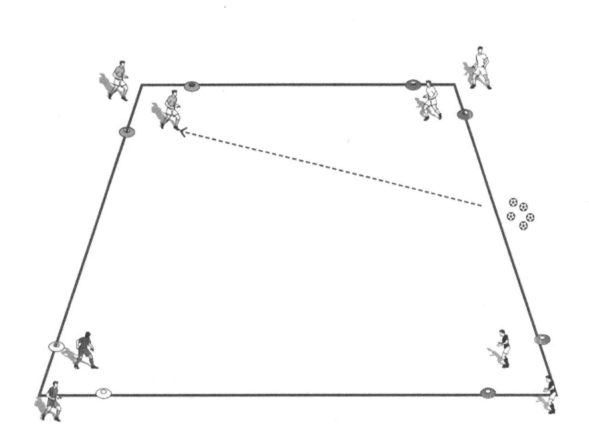

1. 1v1v1v1. Groups of players in each corner with cone goals. The coach passes the ball into one of the players. It is useful to have criteria for choosing who to pass to. That player can then score in any of the goals (apart from his own). This could become a 1v1, 1v2 or 1v3 situation depending on what the player with the ball decides to do, or what the players without the ball decide to do. Do they press the ball? Do they stay on their line? Does the dribbler immediately pick out an individual to attack?
2. Add goalkeepers.
3. Join two teams together. Stripes and black vs. white and green.

6 – Angled Goals

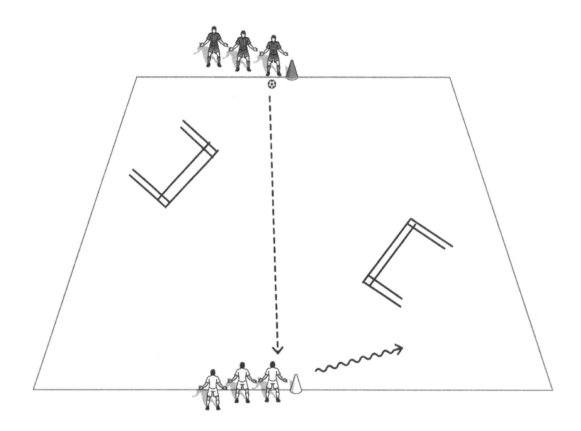

1. A striped player pass to white. There are two goals positioned at offset angles. The player with the ball may score in either of the two goals. The two defenders need to prevent the player from scoring. If the defender wins the ball, they can score in either goal. The angle of the goals means that a good first touch is vital, as is the ability to feint and quickly change direction.

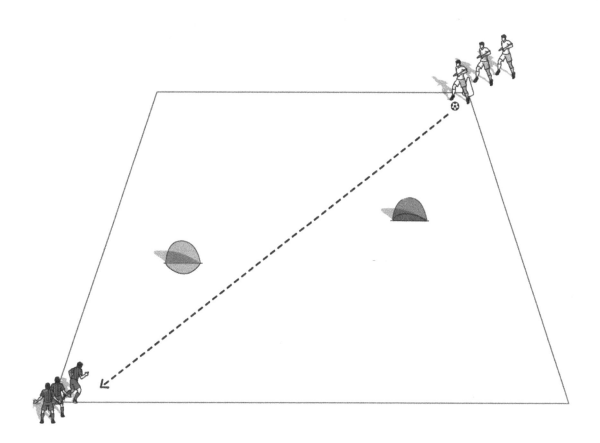

7 – Reversed Goals

1. Stripe passes across to white. White can score in either goal. If the stripe
   wins the ball, they may also score in either goal. The closest goal to the
   player receiving is positioned the wrong way around, making it difficult to
   score an easy goal. The player receiving the ball needs to use speed and
   deception to score. The direction of the goals also affects the defender. It is
   possible for the attacker to score with a quick shot into the far goal. If the
   defender covers that goal quickly, they can score an easy goal themselves.
   The defender needs to work out the best way to protect the goal and still be
   able to apply pressure to the attacker.

8 – Transition 1

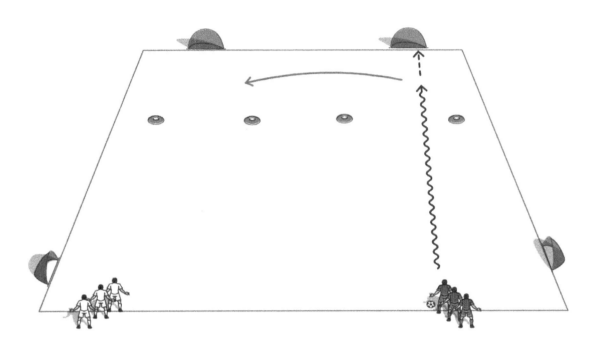

1. A striped player starts. The player with the ball drives forward and looks to score in the mini goal immediately in front of them, but only after crossing the four cone shooting line. As soon as the stripe crosses the line, a white player attacks the goal in front of them. The stripe needs to react quickly after shooting to defend the goal.
2. If the defending player wins the ball, they can score in either of the side goals.
3. Instead of only scoring in the goal immediately in front, the attacking player can attack either goal, thus getting the defender off balance with a quick change of direction.

9 – Through The Gate

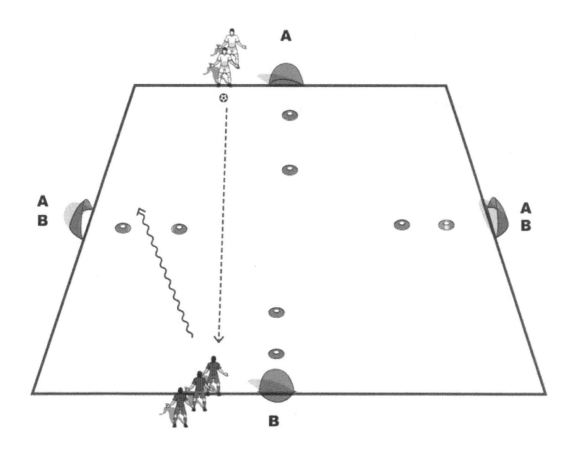

1. White passes to stripe. Stripe receives the ball and attacks any of the goals marked A. The player can only score once they have dribbled through the pair of gates in front of the goal. If white wins the ball, they can score in any goal marked B.
2. Enforce a rule that if the player passes through the cones with the ball on their left foot, it needs to be a left foot finish. If they pass through and the ball is on their right, it needs to be a right foot finish.
3. Play 2v2. The goal can only be scored if the ball has passed through the cones. This may be with a dribble, pass, or first touch.

10 – When to Shoot?

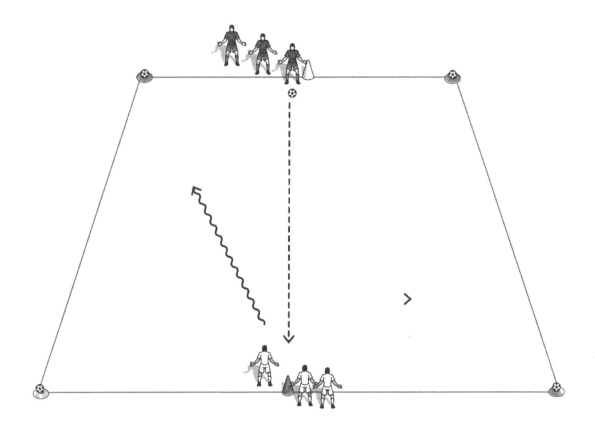

1. Stripe passes the ball to white. White attacks and scores a point by knocking the ball off either corner cone at the stripe's end. If stripe wins the ball, they can score by knocking the ball off either corner cone at the white team's end.
2. Add a halfway line. If the attacking player crosses that line, they have the option of turning and attacking any of the four footballs. Encourage turning, changes of direction, acceleration, deception, and intelligence.

11 – Man Marked 1

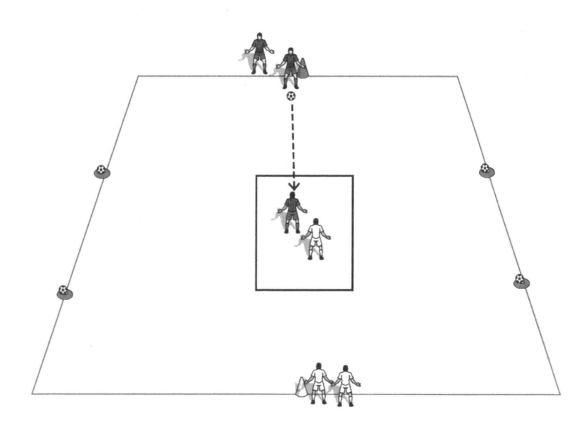

1. Stripe passes the ball into his teammate inside the square. He is under pressure from the white team defender who is also in the square. The aim is for the striped player to get out of the square and knock off any of the balls on cones. If the white player can win the ball, he can knock any of the balls off the cones. Encourage the attacker to use their body and demand where they want the pass. How can the attacker make it difficult for the defender to read where he is going?

12 – Man Marked 2

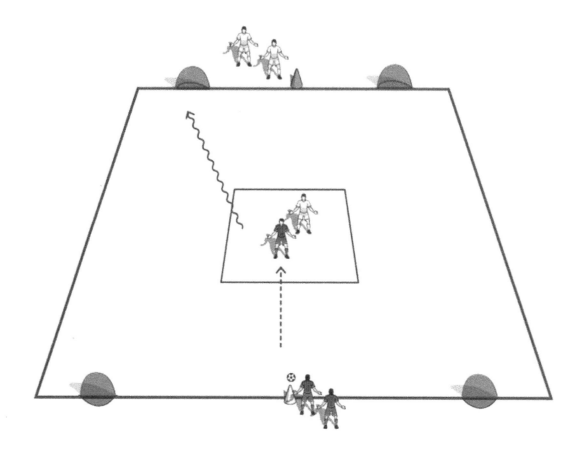

1. Stripe passes to a teammate inside the square. The white defender applies pressure to the stripe and tries to intercept or win the ball in a challenge. Stripe is looking to spin or turn past the defender to then score in either of the mini goals at the white team's end. If the white wins the ball, they can attack and score in either of the mini goals at the striped team's end.
2. Progression. If the stripe turns the white defender, one of the white players at the cone can step out to defend the mini goals. The turned defender can also recover to create a 1v2. Encourage the attacker to finish the movement quickly.

13 – Combining

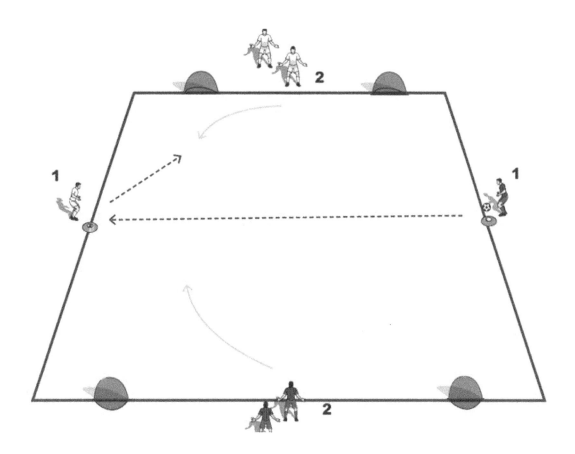

1. Stripe 1 passes to white 1. White 1 sets the ball back to white 2. Stripe 2 moves off the line, and we have a 1v1 between white 1 and stripe 2. White tries to score in either of the mini goals at stripe's end. If stripe wins the ball, he can score in either goal at the white end.
2. The player in possession can now choose to play a 1-2 with their teammate at the side.
3. When player 1 receives, they can choose whether to set, or attack themselves.
4. Play a 2v1 attack.
5. Play 2v1 with stripe 1 recovering onto the pitch to make a 2v2.

14 – Running on to the Ball

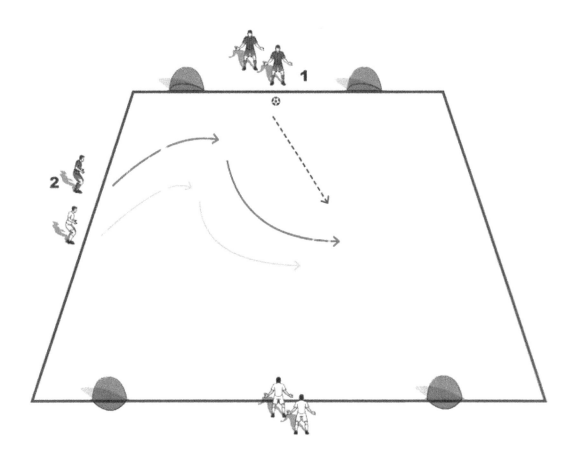

1. An attacker and defender begin on the same side of the area. Stripe 1 waits for stripe 2 to make a move and then makes a pass. The white defender on the side looks to mark the striped attacker. Play 1v1 with stripe able to score in either of the white team's goals. White can score in either striped goal if they win the ball. Encourage movement to receive, forward passes, shielding, and running with the ball.
2. After passing, stripe 1 joins the attack to create a 2v1.
3. The second white defender joins for a 2v2.

15 – Transition 2

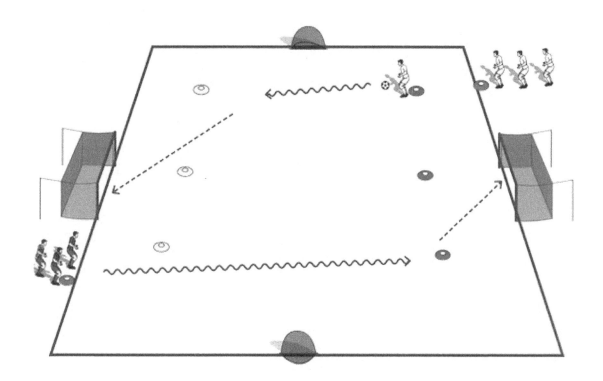

1. Players have a ball each. White starts with the ball and attacks the left-hand goal. Once they are through the three left-hand cone gates, they shoot into an empty net. React, turn, and defend. As soon as white crosses through the left-hand gates, stripe attacks the right-hand goal. Once they cross through the right-hand gates, stripe can shoot. They then need to recover and defend as white will set off once stripe passes through the gate. Should the defender recover in time and win the ball, they can score in either of the goals at the side.
2. Add goalkeepers.

16 – One vs the Goalkeeper

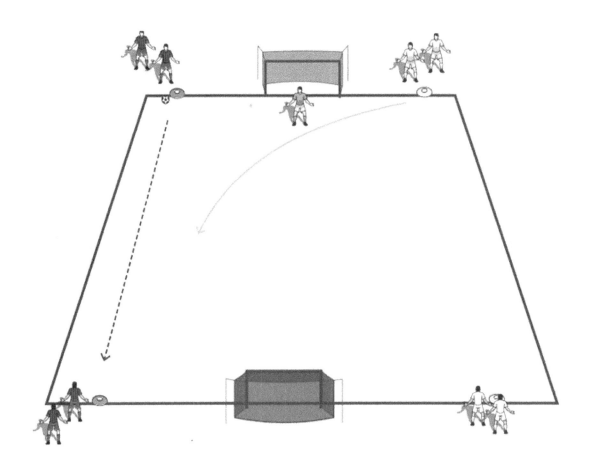

1. Stripe passes to stripe. White moves to close down the striped player before they can shoot at goal. The stripe can take an early shot or try to get closer to the goal before shooting. If they choose to get closer, they may have to take on the defender. If the defender wins the ball, they score in the empty goal. Next turn, white passes to white with a stripe closing down. Encourage good first touches and a willingness to shoot with a non-dominant foot.

17 – Gauntlet

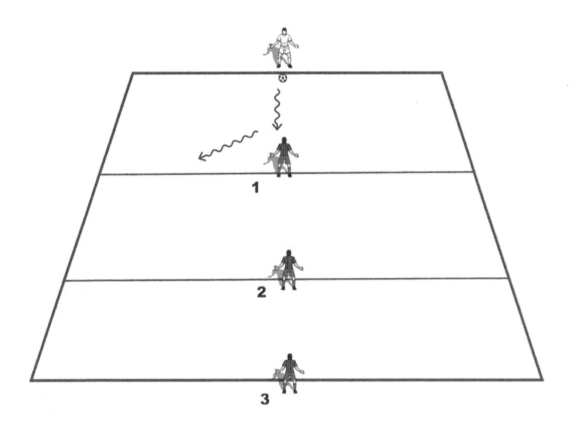

1. Simple 1v1. The white starts with the ball and dribbles against stripe 1. If they pass stripe 1, they then take on stripe 2. If they get past stripe 2, they take on stripe 3. If the defender wins the ball, switch places with the dribbler.

18 – Give and Go

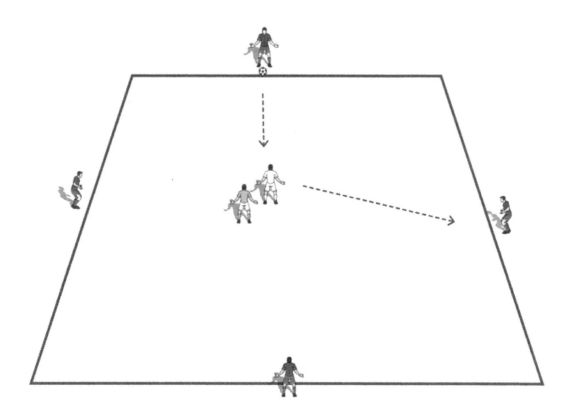

1. Four players positioned around the outside. The two players in the middle play 1v1 against each other on the inside. They use the outside players to help them keep the ball. When a ball is played to an outside player, the outside player needs to try to give the ball back to the player who initiated the exchange. If a pass is not on the outside, players may play one pass to another outside player, to change the angle. Use movement, shielding, and dribbling skills to retain possession. Play for two minutes then switch the middle players.

19 – Space to Shoot

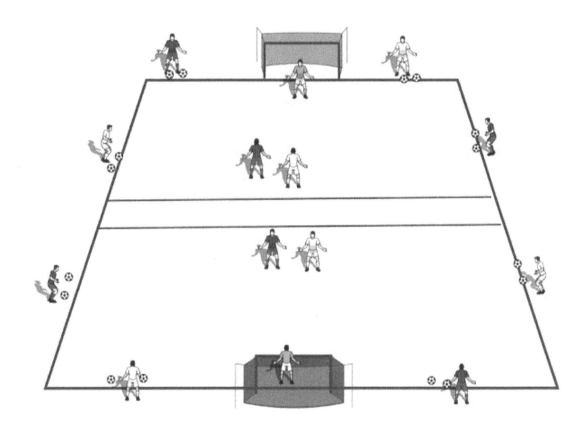

1. Two players play 1v1 in each half. They look to receive passes from their teammate after finding space to shoot. If they cannot find the space, they will have to receive and then create their own space. If the shot is in, or pushed behind by the goalkeeper, they look to receive another ball. If the shot is saved and stays in play, the ball is live until it goes out of play. If the ball goes off the pitch after touching a stripe, it is white ball and vice versa. If the defending player gains possession, they may shoot. Each player receives a maximum of four balls. Play until all the balls have been used.
2. Combine the two pitches and play 2v2 with players able to score in any goal.
3. Make the practice directional so players can only score at one end.

20 – Dribbling Cores

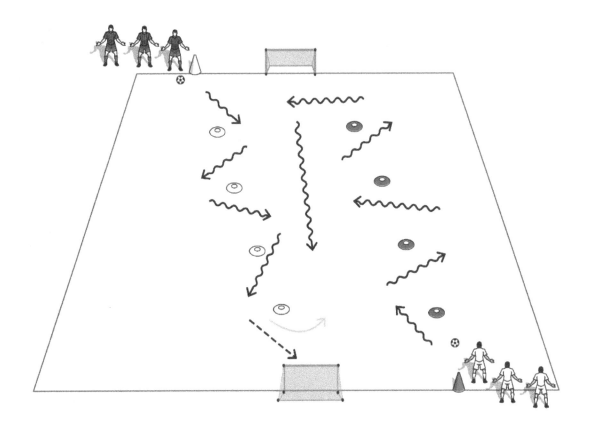

1. Practice core dribbling moves plus 1v1. Both stripe and white dribble in and out of the cones using different parts of the foot. When stripes reach the end, they finish before turning to defend. When whites reach the end, they spin and attack the goal now being defended by a stripe. If the stripe wins the ball, they attack the opposite goal.

21 – Loose Ball Battle

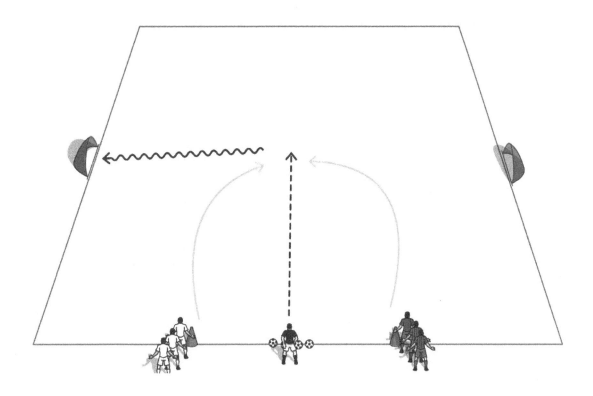

1. The two groups align either side of a coach (or player). The coach passes a ball into the middle. The first player from each group races to the ball to see who gets there first. The player with the ball may score in either goal.

22 – Cutting In

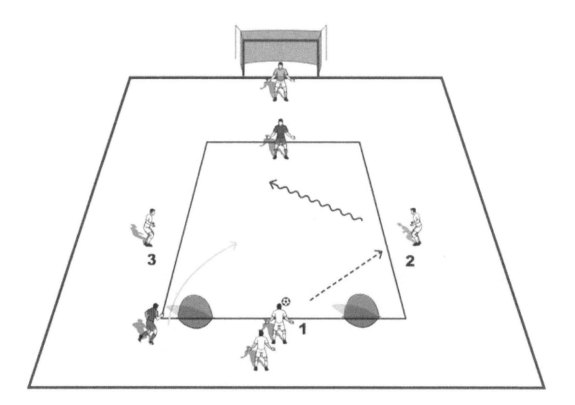

1. White 1 passes to white 2 who cuts in for a 1v1 with the striped defender. The stripe on the line with white 1 makes a recovery run to apply transition pressure. White 2 can take the shot on quickly or attempt to beat the defender. White 1 then takes the space vacated by white 2. The next pass from position 1 will be to white 3. Should the stripes win the ball, they have a 2v1 attack into the mini goals.
2. White must get out of the box before shooting.
3. White must shoot inside the box.
4. White 1 joins the attack to create a 2v2 (when including the recovering defender).
5. White 2 may pass to white 3 to create an attack. White 1 can also join to create a 3v2.

23 – Transition 3

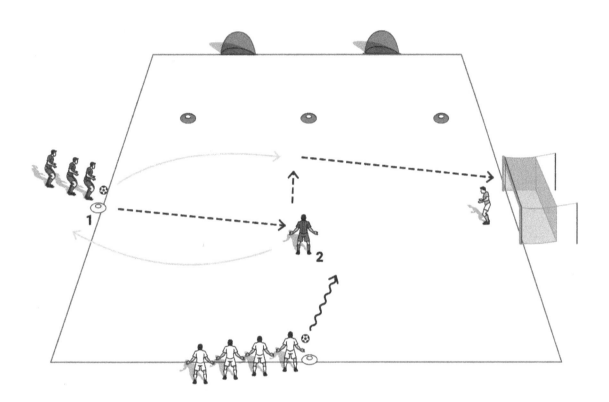

1. Stripe 1 starts with the ball. He plays a 1-2 with stripe 2 and shoots. As soon as the shot is released, the white player attacks the two mini goals. The player who shot has to recover and defend the two mini goals. White can only shoot once past the three cones.
2. Both stripes defend the white player after the 1-2, rather than after the shot.

24 – Side to Side

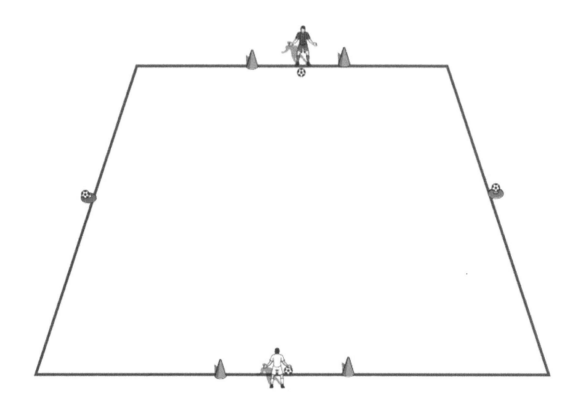

1. Stripe and white have a ball at their feet standing at the gate. They perform a move (toe taps, foot roll, etc.). On the coach's call ("A" or "B"), the players run with the ball to one of the side balls to see who can knock it off first.
2. As above, but players leave their footballs in the goals and race to get a side ball. The player with the ball tries to score in their opponent's goal.

25 – Multiplayer 1v1

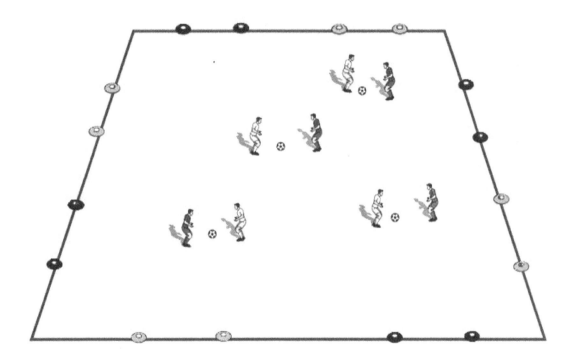

1. Stripe and white face each other 1v1. White can score by dribbling through any grey gate. Stripe can score by dribbling through any black gate. When a goal is scored, restart in the middle. The player who conceded is now on the attack.

26 – Knock It Over

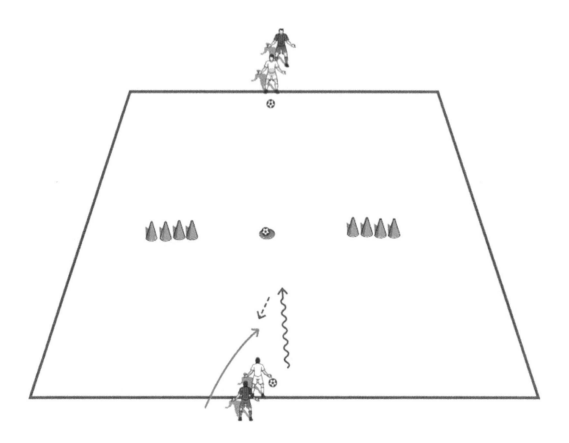

1. White dribbles forward a few steps before heeling the ball to stripe who tries to knock over the cone. One point for knocking over a cone. Three points for knocking the ball off the central cone.

27 – Goal to Goal

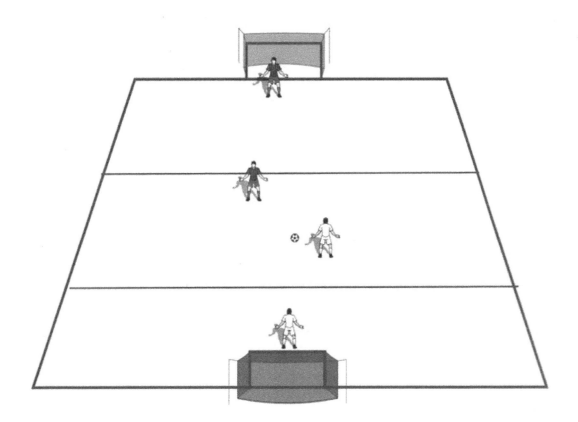

1. Stripe vs. white, 1v1 in the centre, to start. If the attacker beats the defender, they are 1v1 with the sweeper keeper. If the sweeper keeper wins the ball, then they are an attacker and may enter the central zone to create a 2v1 (or 2v0 if the player does not recover). If the 2v1 does not yield a goal, the other sweeper keeper joins the attack to create a 2v2.
2. The team in possession attacks 2v1 with the goalkeeper fixed.
3. The team in possession attacks 2v1 with the forward fixed in the final third.

4
Why 3v3?

Technical development cannot happen without the ball.

Although in the professional game, research shows that players are likely to only have two to four minutes in possession, they must be able to maximise that time with the ball – which means they must have been afforded the time and opportunity to develop their technical actions during training. If our young players spend only two minutes with the ball, during matches, for example, then opportunities are being missed. The obvious answer is to decrease the number of players on the field, during training, which means coaches need to decide how small to make their matches.

In the last 50 years, 4v4 (no goalkeeper) and 5v5 (with a goalkeeper) have been the most common small sided games used. Famously, in Dutch football, 4v4 has been their way. While Liverpool had their spell dominating English football, the players were always asked, "What do you do in training?". The answer would always be, "We play 5-a-side".

My belief is that when we develop our footballers, we should go smaller still.

Technical Actions	3-a-side	4-a-side	5-a-side	Bout 1	Bout 2	Bout 3
Involvements with the ball	31±6	32±4	31±4	33±4	31±5	30±4
Passes	19±4	20±4	22±4	20±3	20±4	19±3
Target passes (%)	73.4±9	75±11	76±9	75.4±6	75.1±8	74±11
Crosses	3±1	1±1	1±1	2±1	2±1	1±1
Dribbling	4±2	2±1	2±1	3±1	3±2	3±1
Shots on goal	3±1	2±1	2±1	2±1	2±1	2±1
Tackles	2±1	2±1	2±2	2±1	2±1	2±1
Headers	1±1	1±1	1±1	1±1	1±1	1±1

± Calculated on 2 sessions

Table taken from the paper, *The Usefulness Of Small Sided Games Training*, by Filipe Manuel Clemente, Micael S. Couceiro, Fernando Manuel Lourenco Martins and Rui Mendes.

The table above shows the number of technical actions per game when small-sided games are used. The numbers, in general, are very similar. The information not displayed is the number of actions per player but simple maths can determine that six players having 31 involvements with the ball will have around five involvements each, while ten players with 31 involvements/passes will have around three involvements each.

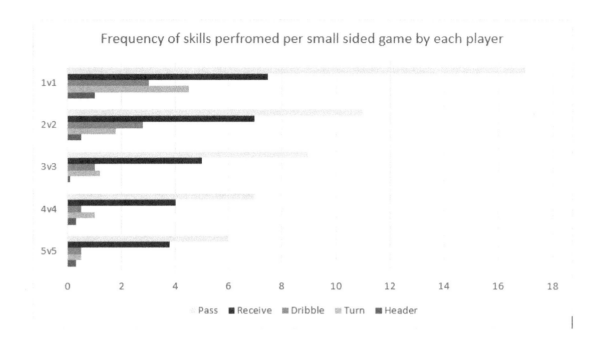

Frequency of skills perfromed per small sided game by each player

"An increase in the number of players performing led to an increase in the total number of technical actions performed. However, the addition of extra players also led to a decrease in the total number of technical actions performed per player." From *Small Sided Games: The Physiological And Technical Effect Of Altering Pitch Size And Player Numbers* by Adam Owen, Craig Twist and Paul Ford. (Graph and quote)

One versus one, and two versus two, encourage significantly more actions per player than even three versus three. These formats lack important elements from football, though. Which is not to say that they are without benefit, particularly one versus one when used in conjunction with three versus three.

Defensive Shapes

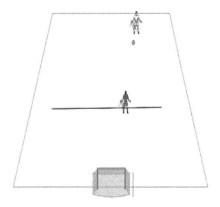

One defender lines of defence

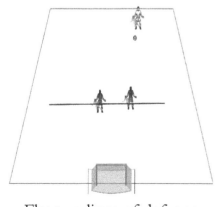

Flat two lines of defence

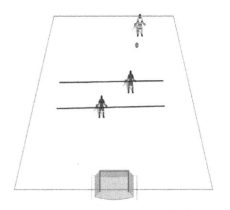

Job and a half lines of defence

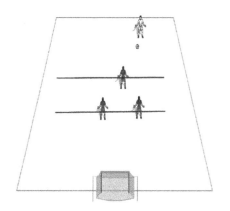

Defensive triangle lines of defence

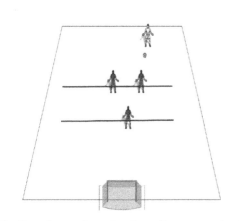

Defensive triangle (set for pressing)
lines of defence

Attacking Shapes

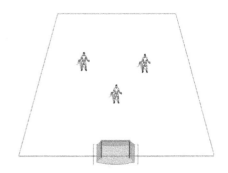

Offensive triangle with one forward

Offensive triangle with two forwards

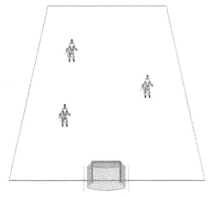

Offset offensive triangle with two in line and one high and wide

Offset attacking triangle with two in line and one deep and wide

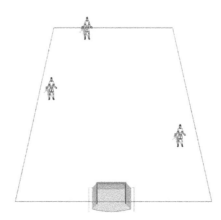

Offset offensive triangle with two deep and one very high and wide

Patterns of Play

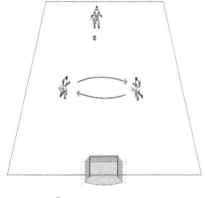

Crossover runs

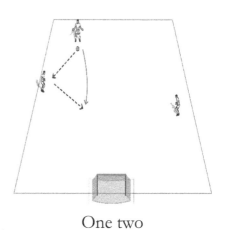

One two

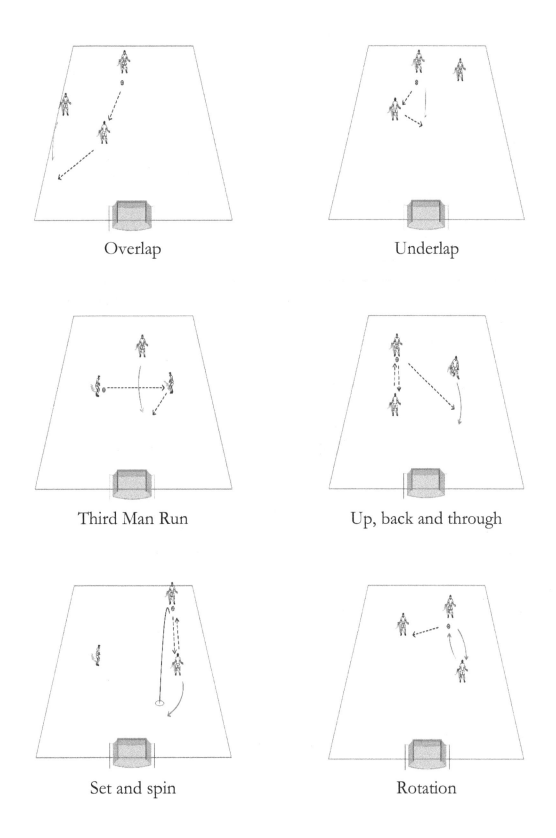

Overlap

Underlap

Third Man Run

Up, back and through

Set and spin

Rotation

All of the above can also happen within 3v3, 4v4 and 5v5, but as previously highlighted, we also want to optimise the number of individual technical opportunities.

"Strategically, 3v3 football uses the smallest tactical unit able to apply the principle of depth and breadth for effective team offence and defence." From *Effective 3-A-*

Chapter 4

Side Game Formats And Team Strategies For Advanced Level by Harry Huball, Ian Franks, Mike Sweeney and Risto Pauppinen.

Each moment with the ball is a possible pass, dribble, or shot. The players not on the ball will all have a strong chance of being involved in the next game action. With young children, I have seen them have very few touches even when playing 4v4 and 5v5. In 3v3 there is no place to hide. The ball will eventually find you; then you need to decide what to do with it. Will you accept the challenge in front of you and take it on? The desire is to have players comfortable in 1v1, 1v2 and 1v3 situations – the 3v3 format of the game creates these, allowing our young players to express themselves and be creative. Will they decide that they are in a position to shoot? The pitch isn't that big, so perhaps the player can hone their finishing abilities and become the goal scorer they have dreamed of being. Or will they spot the movement of a teammate and play the killer pass? Can they master the assist because of the options available in the 3v3 format?

It is my belief that by using 3v3, we will give our players their best opportunity to have the freedom they need to discover who they are, and what they can do, while still learning the core components of football. We give them the chance to become outstanding ball players with good decision making and game knowledge.

Horst Wein was a great proponent of the benefits of a 3v3 format for player development. His ideas began in hockey before moving into football. Wein emphasised the four goal (two per team) format and developed Funinho for young players. This work builds upon the principles started by Horst Wein.

*It is worth noting that not all practices are precisely 3v3 and may be better described as 6 player practices. These can easily transition into a 3v3 game.

1 – Small-Sided Free Play

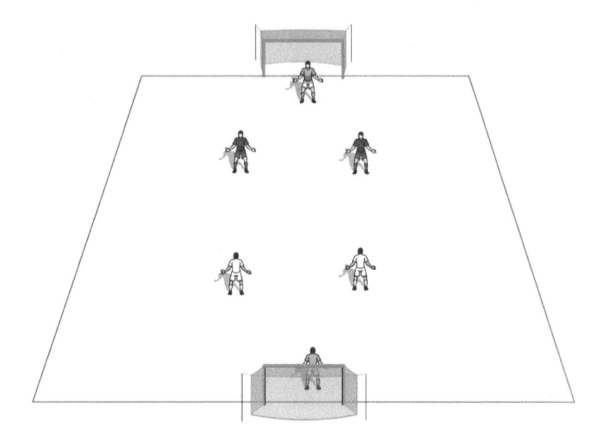

Ensure that the pitch is small enough that the goalkeepers can shoot and be involved in the general play.

2 – Four Goal Game

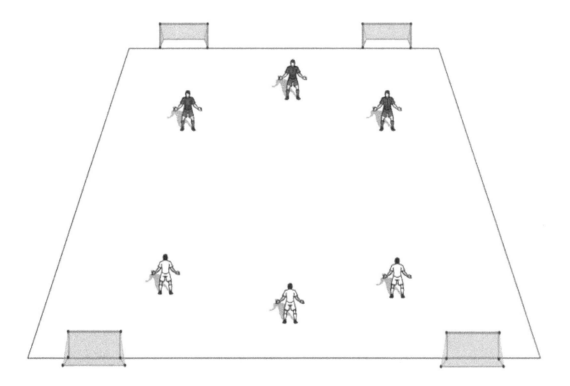

Encourage the use of space and increased opportunities to score.

Discourage players from just defending the goal (though let them try initially, as it may create 1v1 situations).

Look for the players' spacing and opportunities to switch play.

3 – Target Players

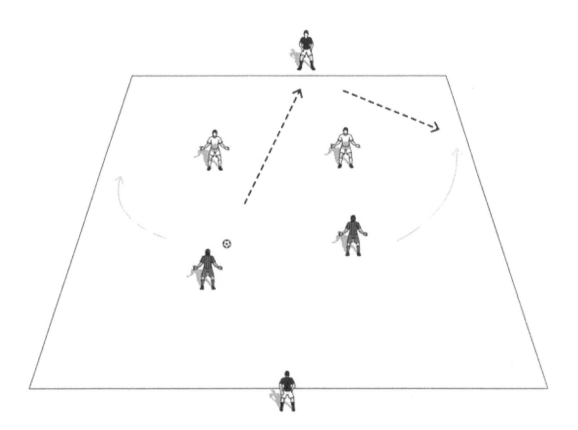

2v2 + 2.

A team scores a point each time they play into one of the end players. After playing in, look to move and receive a pass. Turn and play into the target player at the opposite end. Continue playing from end to end until the opposition win possession.

Coaching Points

- Body shape
- Orientated first-touch
- Fast passing
- Movement to find space
- Types of move (1-2, overlap, up back and through, etc.)

4 – Two vs Two plus Two

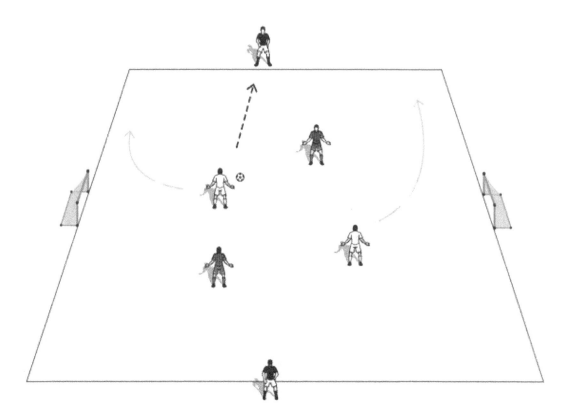

The white team looks to play from target player to target player in order to score points. If stripes win the ball, they can break away and score in either of the two goals. The white team may try to win back possession.

After a set period of time, switch the team roles.

Coaching Points

- Passing
- Movement
- Set moves (1-2, overlap, etc.)
- Transition
- Counter-attack
- Running with the ball

5 – Four vs Two Possession

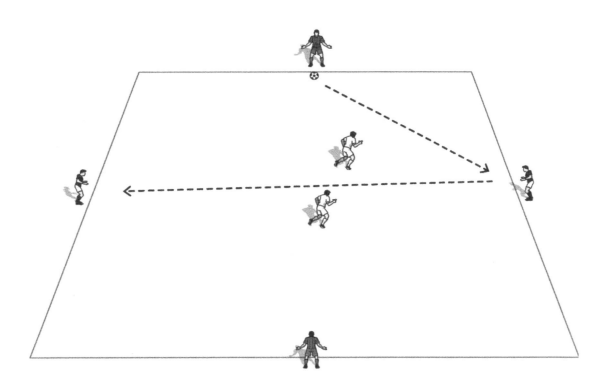

The players are in pairs so that if a player gives the ball away they, and their partner, switch with the middle two players.

Coaching Points

- Fast passing (one- and two-touch)
- Quality of pass
- Small amounts of movement to create support and passing angles
- Teamwork and pressing from the middle two – do not allow a splitting pass

6 – Support Players

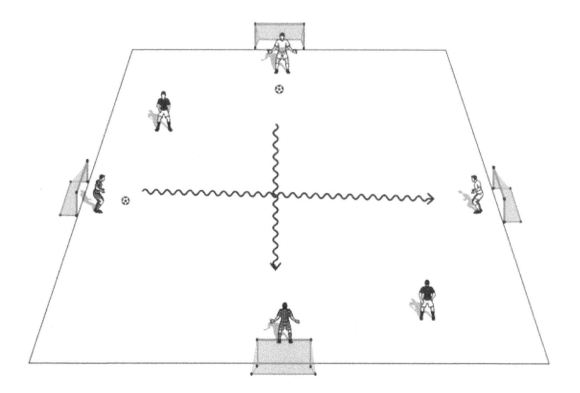

1v1 & 1v1 with two neutral players.

Two 1v1s take place simultaneously. The two neutral players can be used by anyone who has possession.

The 1v1 starts after the player with the ball plays a 1-2 with a neutral player.

The neutral players could decide to both help the same player, creating 3v1 for one mini-game while the other mini-game stays at 1v1.

Coaching Points

- Dribbling moves
- Combinations
- Communication
- Awareness
- Movement

7 – In Zones - Vertical

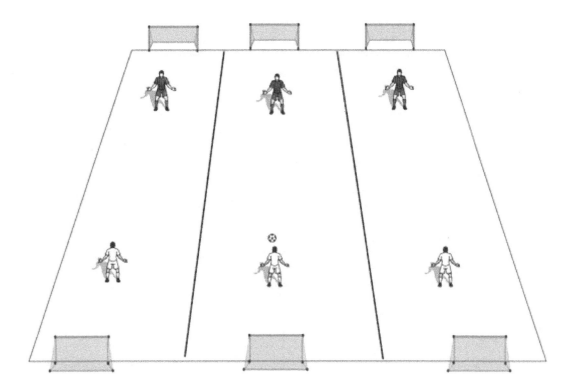

Locked into zones.

Start with three x 1v1.

Progress to one ball with the players locked into their zones but able to score in any goal.

How does this affect the way the players defend?

Allow attackers to follow their passes and create attacking overloads. Attackers might even choose to follow the ball into the zone they passed into, but make a run in behind.

Coaching Points

- Dribbling
- Finishing
- Combining
- Movement

8 – Midfielder Game

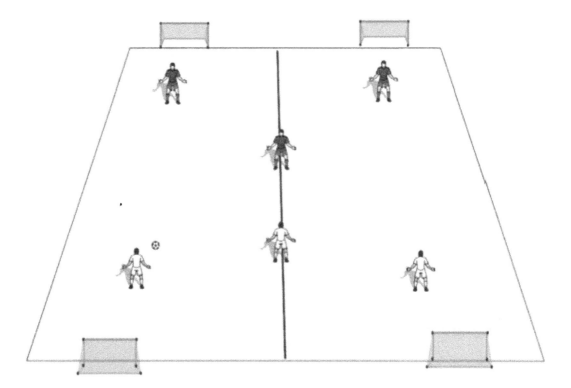

Two players from each team are locked into their half of the pitch. One player from each team is free to move from zone to zone. They are the midfielder, and they help with attacking and defending.

Coaching Points

- Decision making for the midfielder. Who to help? Where to support?
- Awareness
- Movement
- 1v1
- 2v1
- 2v2
- Cover and balance

9 – Midfielder Game 2

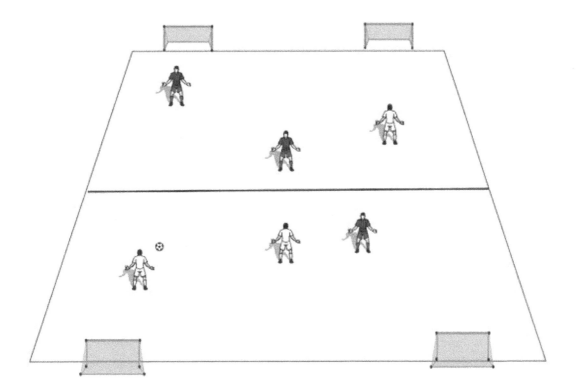

Two players from each team are locked into each half of the pitch. One player from each team is allowed to move from half to half. They are the midfielder and help with attacking and defending.

Progress to rotation. No player is fixed, but one player must remain in each half at all times.

Coaching Points

- Decision making for midfielder
- Awareness
- Movement
- Communication

10 – One Touch Finish

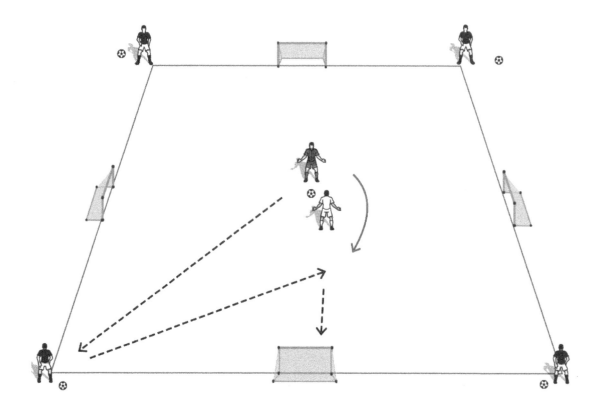

The two central players face each other. They can score in any goal, but it must be a one-touch finish following a pass from an outside player (outside players have a two-touch maximum). If a player scores, they get another ball until they miss or their opponent intercepts.

Coaching Points

- Movement
- Combination
- Finishing
- Decision making – When to pass? When to hold? When to dribble and why?

11 – One Touch Finish 2

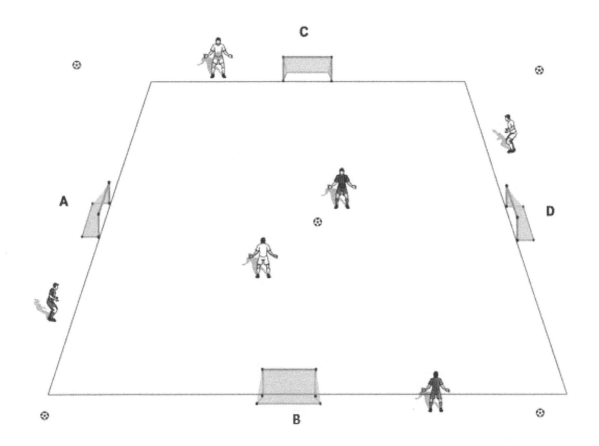

Stripes can score in goal A or goal B.

Whites can score in goal C or goal D.

Players can score with a one-touch finish after passing to a teammate and getting the return.

After a goal is scored, the player who didn't score restarts with the ball.

Coaching Points

- Movement
- Combining
- Finishing

12 – Three Player Transition

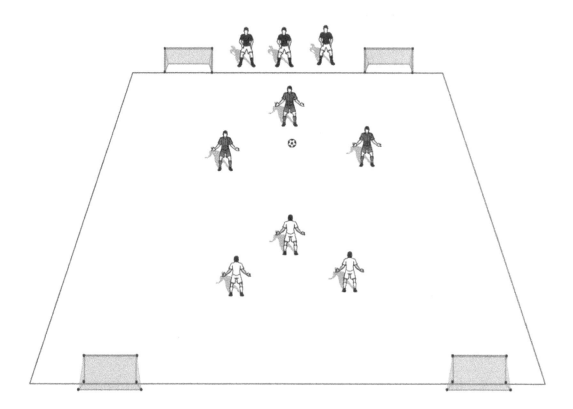

The striped team attacks against the white team. As soon as the stripes lose the ball, the white team attacks the black team. The stripes get off the pitch and occupy the space on the line behind the goal which the whites had initially defended.

If the white team win possession, the attack starts immediately. If the ball leaves the pitch, the coach gives them a ball to start the attack. Allow the teams to choose if they want to play with three outfield players when defending, or two and a goalkeeper.

Progression

- If the attacking team scores, they get another attack and turn to attack the opposite end. This continues until they lose the ball.

Coaching points

- Fast attacks
- Movement
- Support
- Finishing

13 – End Zones

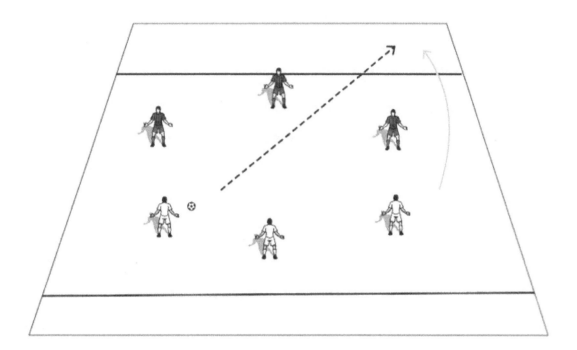

To score a point, dribble into the opponent's end zone or play a forward pass for a teammate to run onto and receive in the end zone.

Coaching Points

- Movement
- Combination moves
- Dribbling/running with the ball
- Transition

14 – Diamond Shooting

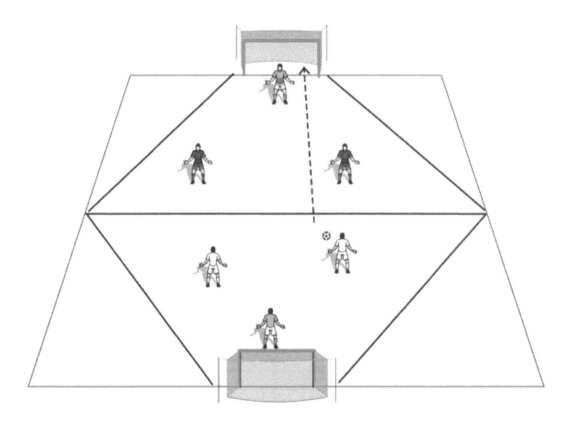

Goal to goal.

Players are locked into their own half. All players can shoot.

Progression – allow one player from each half to enter the opposition's half with a dribble or from a forward pass.

Coaching Points

- Types of finish
- Shooting technique(s)
- Awareness of opposition positions and shooting opportunities

15 – Ice Hockey

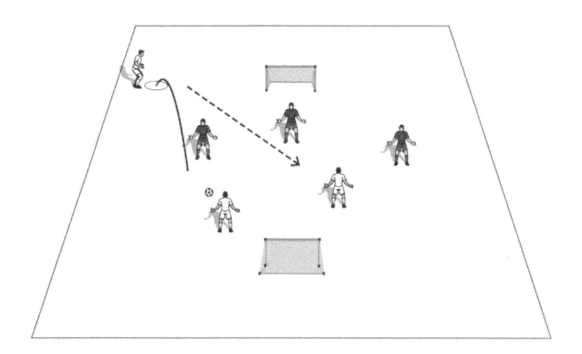

Goals are positioned so that there is a good amount of space behind them. Players are able to go behind the goals by dribbling or moving to receive.

Coaching Points

- Awareness of the positions of team mates relative to the goals
- Movement
- Lifted passes
- Through passes
- Creation of angles

16 – Reversed Goals

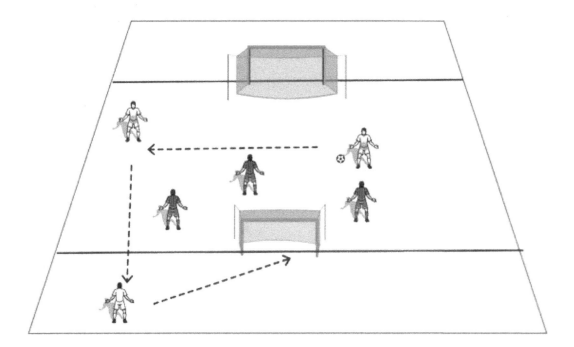

Goals and inside end zones. Players can make runs into the end zones to receive and finish.

Progress to allow a recovering defender to enter the end zone. Another player can enter the end zone after the pass to create a 2v1.

Alternatively, start with a player already in the end zone.

Coaching Points

- Movement
- Combination
- Finishing
- Support
- Killer passes

17 – Attacking Wave 1

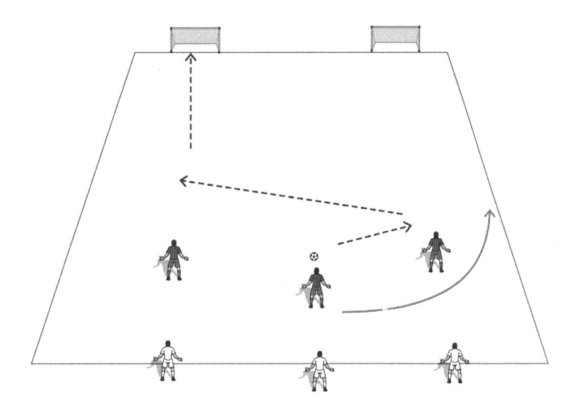

3v0 attack playing one- and two-touch until a player finishes. Look to attack smoothly.

Coaching points

- Fast passing
- Specific movements (overlaps, 1-2s, looping runs)

18 – Attacking Wave 2

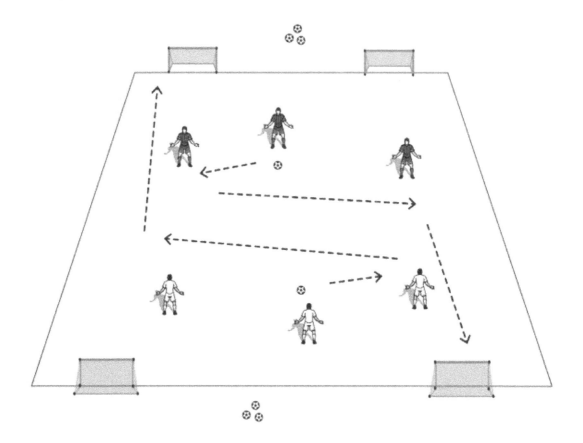

Whites attack one end. Stripes attack the other end. Both attacks happen at the same time. The two teams need to be aware of interference and play through, and around, the other team.

Coaching Points

- Movement
- Fast passing
- Runs
- Support
- Awareness

19 – Attacking Wave 3

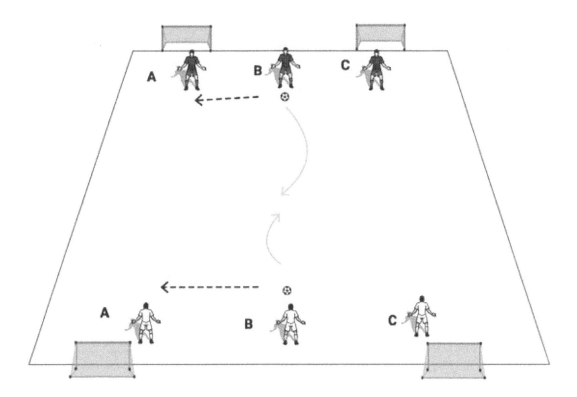

Player B passes to player A and then moves into a defensive position. The attack is 2v1.

Both attacks happen at the same time.

When the attack is over, the players shift one position (A to B, B to C, C to A).

Coaching Points

- Dribbling and running with the ball
- Combination play
- Forwards runs of decoy runs

20 – Attacking Wave 4

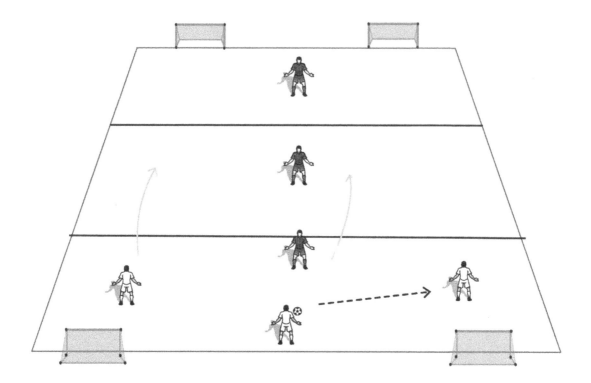

Three zones. One defender locked in each zone. The attackers play through each zone to try to score. If a defender wins the ball, all three can attack the goals behind the white players together.

Add a condition that each attacker must touch the ball at least once in each zone before progressing.

Coaching points

- Combinations
- Triangles
- Movement
- Patience
- Defenders positioning and covering

21 – Attacking Wave 5

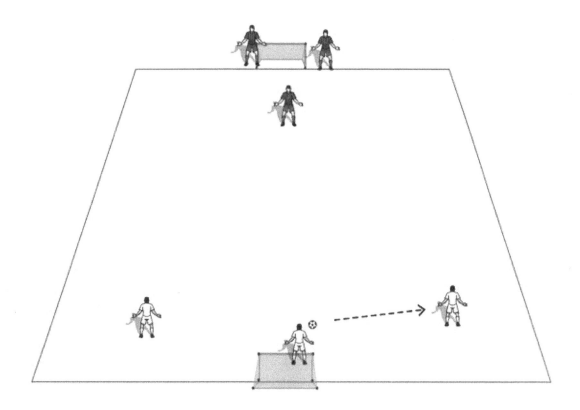

3v1 attack. If the defender wins the ball, his two teammates join to attack and counter in a 3v3. After the white team attack is over, the stripes attack 3v1.

Coaching points

- Movement
- Support
- Attacking moves (1-2, overlap, etc.)
- Dribbling and running with the ball (engage the defender before releasing)

22 – Counter-Punch

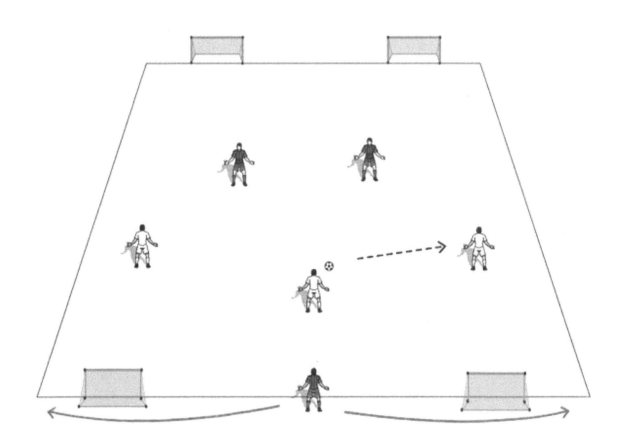

3v2 attack with a counter-attacking outlet.

If the two defenders win the ball, they will have an option to play a forward pass and then make a quick forward run. The receiving player lays the ball off for a one-touch finish.

How does this affect the way the white team attack 3v2? Do they need to be conscious of keeping a player in a defensive position even while attacking?

The target player needs to move to find the most effective space.

23 – Recovery Runs

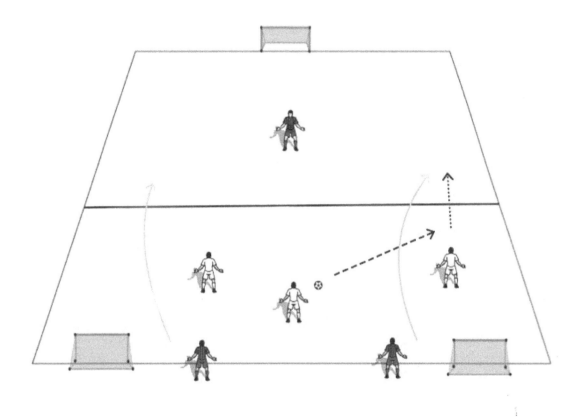

3v1 attack. Once the attackers cross the halfway line, the two players are triggered to recover.

Can the one player delay the attack long enough for the two recovering defenders to get into position to help?

Progression – change the trigger. Use a time limit or make the trigger the first pass from the white team.

Coaching points

- The positioning of the defenders to delay
- The distance of the defenders from attackers
- Angles of recovering players' runs

24 – Forward Passes, Forward Movement

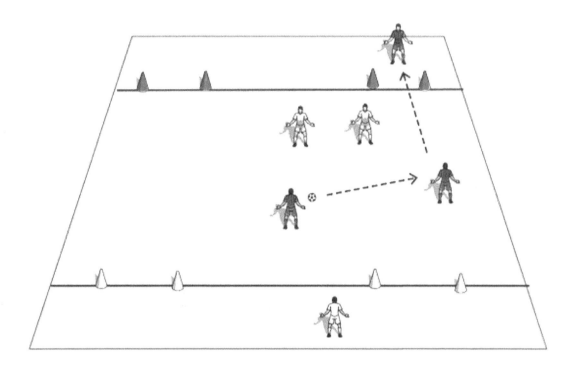

2v2 play centrally. The aim is for the central two to play through the gate to their teammate to score a point.

Progression – Allow the target player to drop into the central area and create a 3v2 attack which allows a player to dribble through the gate to score a point.

Coaching point

- Movement
- Angles
- Quick combinations
- Killer passes

25 – Press

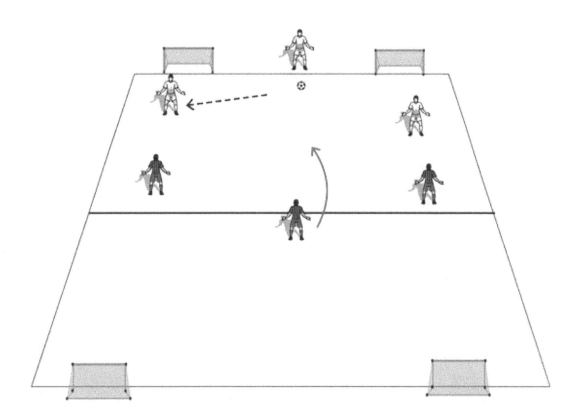

The ball starts with a white player on the edge of the pitch. Before he passes, one of the stripes must be in their own half. Once the pass is played, the stripe steps up.

Can the stripes apply enough pressure to prevent the white team from getting out of their half?

Can the white team play out and score?

Coaching points

- Coordination between the pressing players
- Setting traps and making play predictable
- Distances between pressing players
- Making ground quickly

26 – Press and Cover

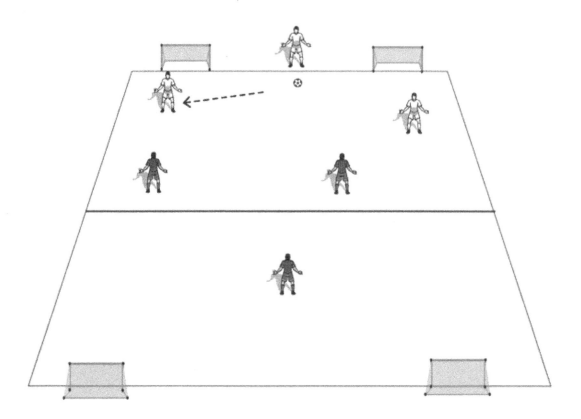

Two players press high with the remaining stripe sweeping behind.

Can the two players direct the play in such a way that they can win the ball?

Can the one covering player look for opportunities to intercept passes or pick up loose balls?

Coaching points

- The timing of when to press
- Target who to press
- Look for press triggers (poor touch, lofted pass, negative pass, engagement with the touchline)

27 – Bounce Passers

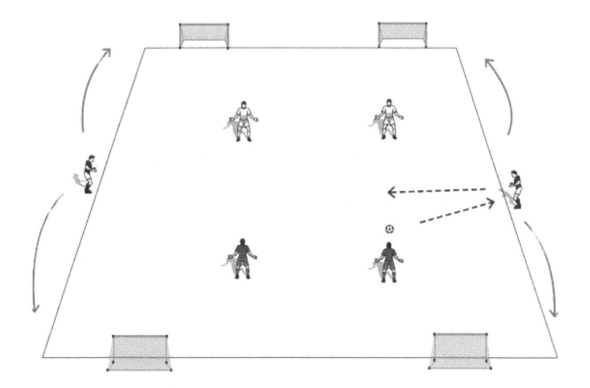

2v2 with two neutral players wide. The neutral players can play one- or two-touch. Neutral players can move anywhere along their line.

If the wide players are not being used, add a rule where a goal cannot be scored unless one of the neutral players has touched the ball within the attacking move. A further rule would be that both neutral players have to touch the ball before a goal can be scored.

Coaching points

- Combinations
- Overloads
- Switching
- Underlaps
- Third man runs

28 – Wide Rotation

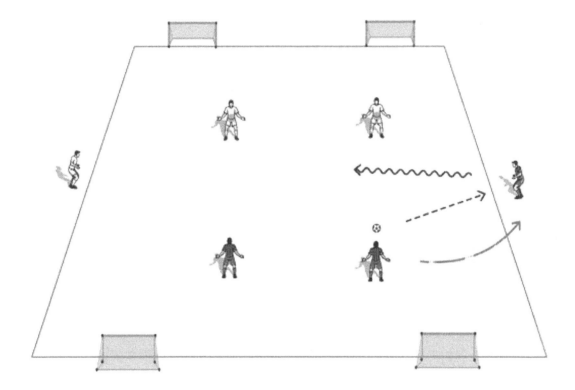

2v2 in the middle. Both teams have a player in a wide position.

If they pass to their wide player, the player who passed takes up the wide position, and the receiving player comes onto the pitch from the wide position.

Progressions

- The wide player must touch the ball before a goal can be scored.
- The player who passes the ball wide can rotate onto either end line or the opposite wide position, not just the position of the player he passed to.

29 – Splitting Passes

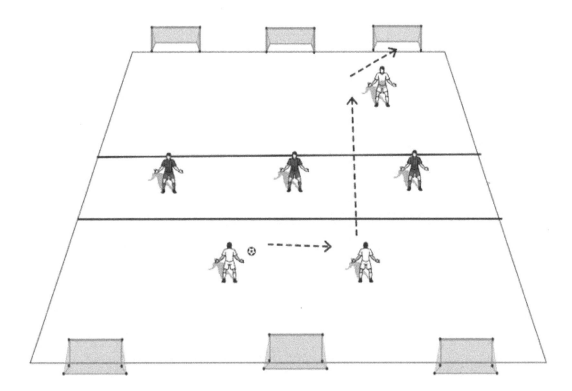

Whites versus stripes. The striped team are locked into the middle section until the moment they win possession.

Can the two white players pass the ball on the floor through the striped players so that their teammate can score? (If they struggle to play through, allow lifted passes).

If the stripes win the ball, they counter-attack and score.

Progressions

- Movement from the whites to disrupt the stripes (dropping into the central zone to allow a 1-2).
- The white team may break the striped line with a dribble.

Coaching points

- Positioning of stripes
- Distances between stripes

30 – Killer Moment

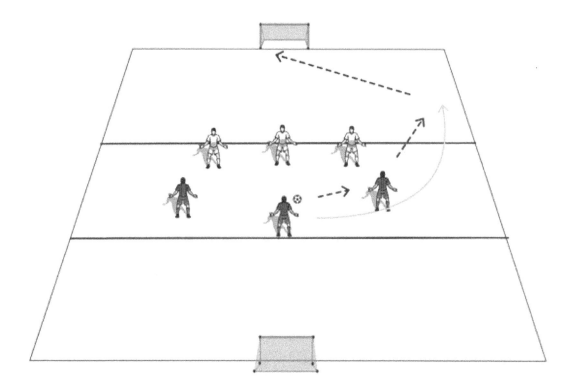

3v3 in a tight midfield area.

Can the team in possession play into the end zone and score?

They can get through with a dribble, or pass into an on-running teammate.

Progression

- Allow one player to drop deep into their own zone to create a passing option in a pocket of space behind the play.

Coaching points

- Combinations
- Angles
- Rotations

31 – First to Four

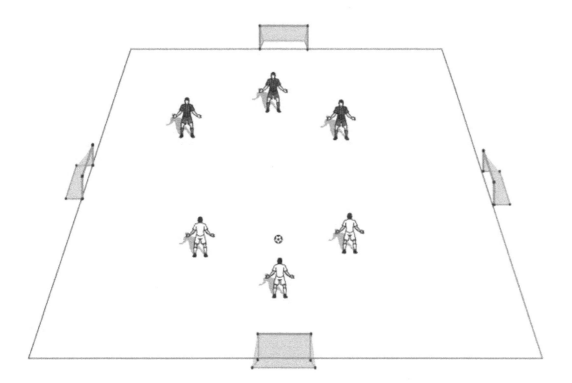

First team to score in all four goals wins. Once a goal has been scored, you do not need to score in it again.

Coaching points

- Awareness
- Movement
- Support
- Imagination
- Creativity
- Transition

32 – Magic Square

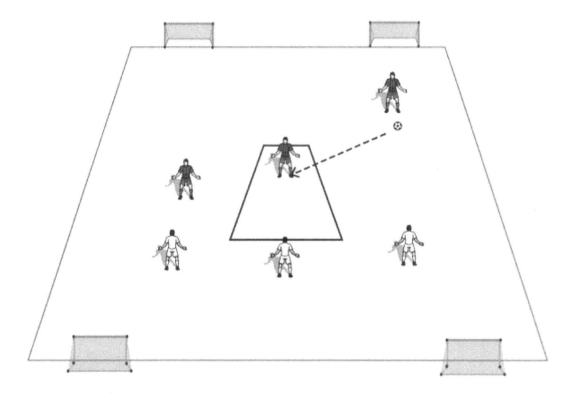

The ball needs to pass through the magic square before the team in possession score. No player should stay in the square.

This could be

- A player dribbling through the square
- A player receiving in the square
- A pass bisecting the square

33 – Defend The Middle

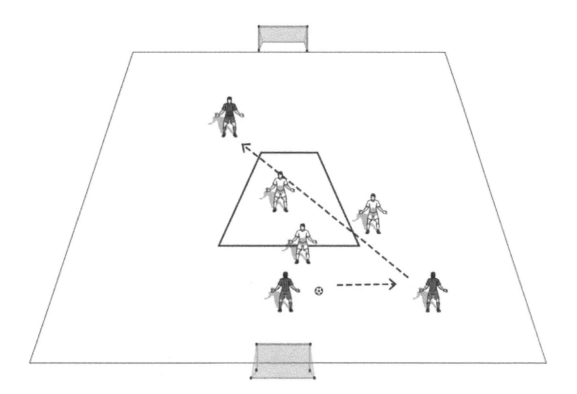

The striped team try to play through the square to score a point.

The white team look to stop the ball going through, and force an interception. If the white team wins the ball, they break away to score in either goal.

Coaching points

- Distances
- Communication
- Discipline
- Concentration
- Adjustment to defend as the angles change

34 – Through The Gates 3v3

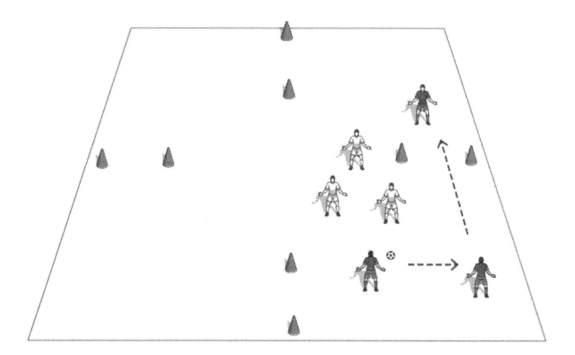

Whites vs stripes. Both teams score a point every time they play through a gate. Play through with either a pass or a dribble.

Coaching points

- Positioning
- Possession
- Angles
- Movement

35 – Quick Transitions

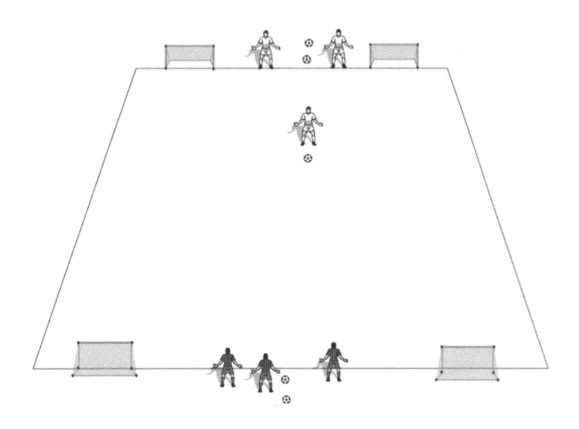

1v0 attack from the white player.

Immediate 2v1 attack from the stripes.

Immediate 3v2 attack from the whites.

Follow with a 1v0 from stripes to start a new sequence.

Alternative sequence. 1v0. 1v1. 2v1. 2v2. 3v2. 3v3.

5
Breaking The Rules

Three versus three is the foundation of our practice, but it is born out of the desire to create dribblers with game understanding. Ultimately, our choice of practice is not driven by our favourite numbers but by principles.

As coaches, we do not always know how many players will turn up. We do not know if our goalkeeping coach is available and whether goalkeepers will be added into any session. We need to be flexible, therefore, and have plans to fall back on. If our goalkeepers are working with the outfield players, the simplest way to include them is to add them to our 3v3, allowing a smooth transition from 3v3 work and then onto a game with increased numbers. The practice will largely be the same for the outfield players, just with the triangles being made in slightly higher positions and the possibility of a fourth point being added, forming a diamond.

We can take similar steps with additional outfield players. If a seventh player arrives to disrupt our perfect 3v3, that player can be added in to make a joker or magic man without changing the objectives too greatly. It may even help a practice that is geared towards overloads when in possession.

Although this book focuses on 3v3 and six player practices, it is important to recognise that it is not the only way to work. To only work on 3v3 throughout a player's development would deny them the opportunity to practice additional aspects of football.

The reasoning behind 3v3 is to maximise touches and utilise the *core shape* in football – the triangle. Adding a player creates a diamond or square. Once you move on from these shapes, offshoots appear which create further triangles or diamonds but, more importantly, fresh options further away from the ball. The sacrifice will be technical (to increase the tactical) but provided we adhere to these shapes, larger numbers will tie into a 3v3 philosophy.

Sometimes it is good just to change up practices. Sometimes we have to break our own rules in order to maintain our principles.

1 – 3v3 Waves + Goalkeepers

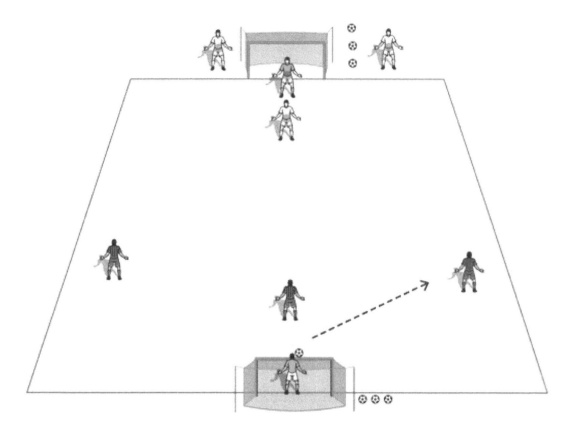

Stripes have three attacks. Then whites have three attacks.

The GK serves to any stripe.

Stripes attack whites 3v1. Then attack 3v2, then 3v3. If the white team wins the ball, they attack the stripes (1v3, 2v3, 3v3).

After the three attacks, switch the team that starts the attack.

Coaching points

- What combinations and movements are possible?
- Attacks need to be at speed.
- How many touches are needed?
- Can players switch positions to make defending more difficult?

2 – Forward Runs

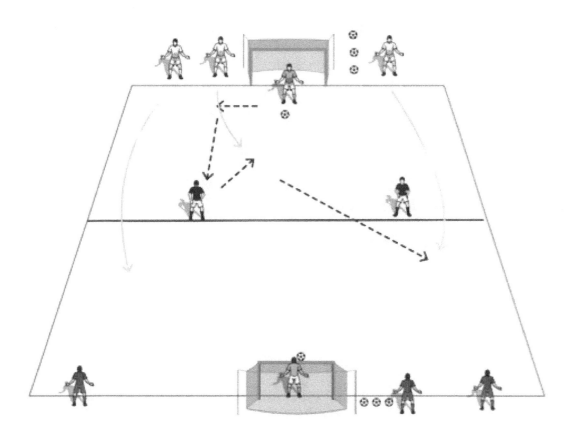

The goalkeeper serves to the side of his goal with two players. The receiving player feeds into the target player on the halfway line. The two players without the ball make forward runs beyond the target player. The solo player moves to receive a pass that has been set back to him by the target player. He can then play forward to either of the runners. Start with attacks alternating from either end. Then progress to both ends starting their attacks at the same time. Use the halfway line as an offside line for the forward runners. Can they curve their runs to stay onside?

Progression

- The passing player does not join the attack and hangs back to act as a defender against a 3v1 attack.

Coaching points

- Make sure to set the ball, and ensure forward passes are angled.
- Paint pictures for different types of finish based on position, angle, goalkeeper position, and where a teammate is.
- Can you take out the goalkeeper so that a teammate can finish easily?

3 – Overloaded Attacks

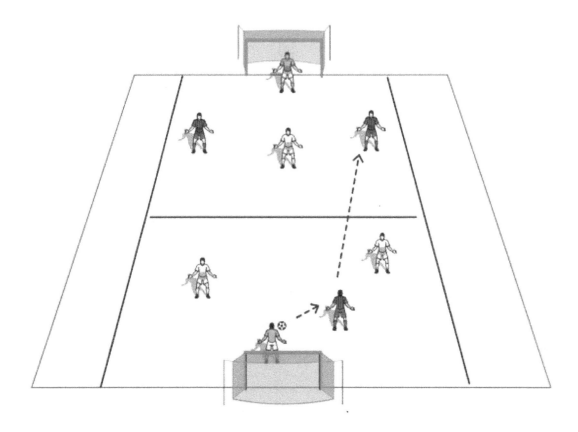

Set up 2v1 for the attackers' advantage in each half.

The goalkeeper feeds the ball to the defender or straight into an attacker to start the attack. If the defender wins the ball, they launch a counter attack.

Attacks start at alternate ends.

Switch round to 2v1 in favour of the defenders. Defenders can join to create 2v2 or 3v2 (but they will be exposed at the back).

Coaching points

- Fast combination play.
- One-twos, overlaps, underlaps, forward passes, set and spin.

4 – Overloaded Attacks 2

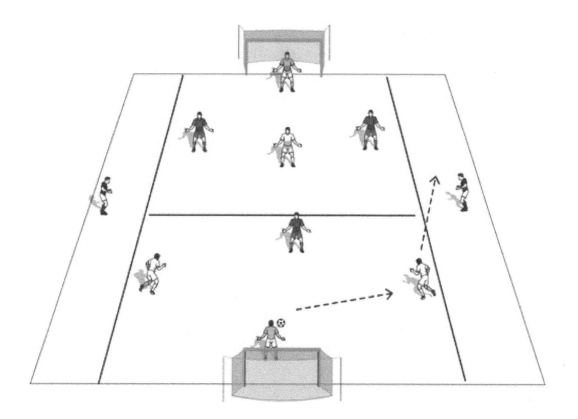

Two against one in favour of the defenders. However, there are wide players who are available. Defenders can join the attacks. The wide players must move up and down to support the attacks.

The wide players are able to score. The wide positions should not be so wide that they can't realistically shoot. The forwards need to find positions from which they can score.

A touch limit for the wide players may be needed to keep things flowing.

Coaching points

- Use the overload.
- Look for quick combinations.
- What are the best scoring positions?
- How can we best serve the forward(s)?
- Prioritise one-touch finishes.

5 – Spatial Awareness

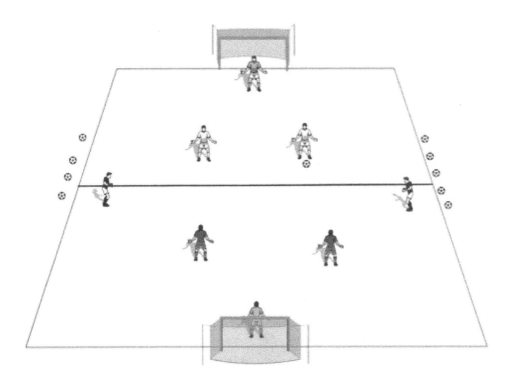

Three against three plus two neutral players. Neutral players can go anywhere on the pitch and can score. After a goal is scored, or an attack ends, get a ball from either side. If you score, get another ball and attack again; the team that was defending (stripes) gets any ball from the side to attack.

Ensure that each team has a turn as the neutral players.

Progression

- Make play non-directional, so attackers are able to score in either goal. In this case, if the goalkeeper gets the ball, they play to the team who did not take the shot. The team cannot attack that goalkeeper until they have crossed the halfway line and turned back.

Coaching points

- Combinations.
- Finishing.
- Movement.
- Forward runs.
- Spatial recognition.

6 – One vs One in the Middle

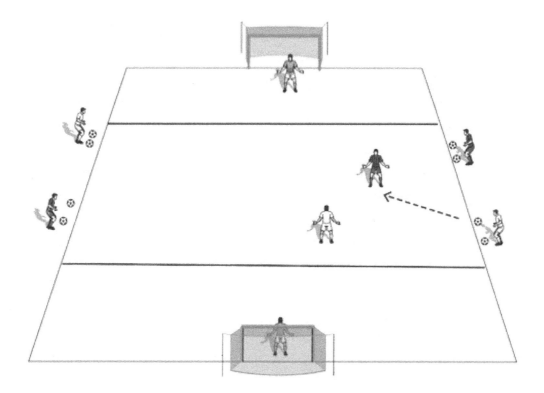

The middle player can only receive a pass from their own teammate. The middle player can finish in any goal. If they score, they receive another ball from their teammate. If they do not score, the player who was defending receives a ball and attacks, or can score with the ball that is live should that ball not go out of play after a shot, tackle, block or intercepted pass.

Progressions

- Use the lines as a shooting line to encourage shots from further out.
- Use the lines as an area from which to finish inside with one touch.
- Outside players serve with a lofted or clipped delivery.
- Make the game directional so players can only attack one end.

Coaching points

- First touch to set up a shot.
- Recognise picture for finish.
- Movement off the ball to find space.

7 – Link with Wide Players

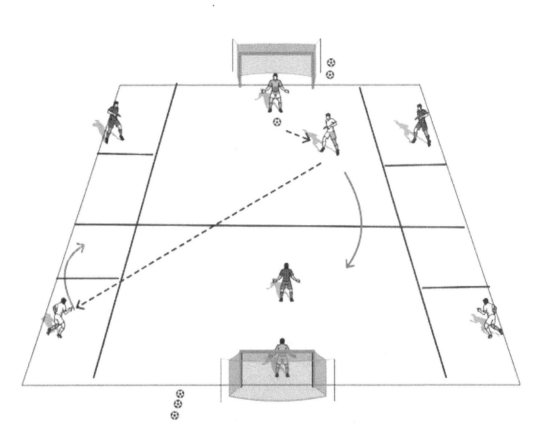

The goalkeeper plays to a central player. The central player can play 1v1 against their opponent or pass to either of their teammates in the wide positions. Look for the corner players to make checked runs from the corner box into the box by the halfway line.

After the corner player receives the ball, they can cut in to attack or drive down the line. The opposite side's forward stays in their box to retain width. They can move in to receive a far post finish.

Attack from alternate ends.

Coaching points

- Decision making – play forward quickly? Take on the opponent? Shoot? Cross? Cut in?
- Checked movement to receive.
- Could the central player move to play up against the defender?
- Look to score as quickly as possible.

8 – Back to back + 3

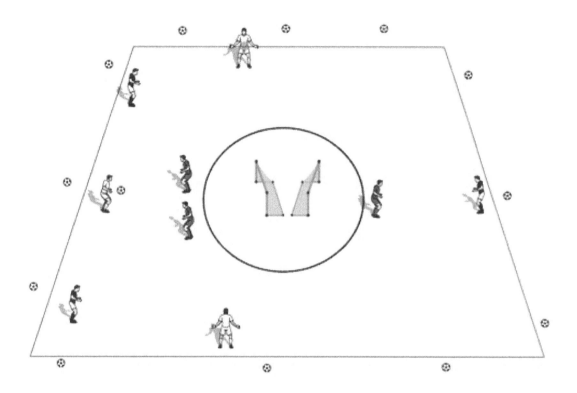

Three whites vs three stripes plus three jokers.

The defending team cannot go inside the circle.

Play starts and restarts from the sides. The team that conceded starts with the ball.

Progressions

- Remove the circle.
- Switch two of the three jokers for goalkeepers (or just add two goalkeepers).

Coaching points

- Movement
- Awareness of space
- Combinations
- Finishing
- Imagination
- Creativity

6
Pitch Types

The great advantage of 3v3 is the number of actions that take place within a small space. The disadvantage is that the 3v3 is only played in a small space.

Eventually players need to be able to work the ball out from the small space and into a full-sized pitch's wide open spaces. While football has become even more technically-dependent, and the very best players are those who can dominate their small spaces, teams have to be able to recognise the spaces that the opposition leaves. With the trend towards teams pushing up high, players must be able to use the space behind the opposition – with a line pass or a diagonal pass – that exploits the weak side. In other words, draw the opposition in close with short passes before playing out to the spaces they have left behind. If teams are playing in low blocks then players have to be able to use the width to overload teams, put crosses into the far post, or play the ball in low and early. Or they need to be exceptional individuals capable of isolating and eliminating opponents.

Defensively, players have to be able to deal with long passes. If they cannot handle a ball travelling a long distance then teams will score a lot of very easy goals. However, technically-capable players are, if they want to be successful defenders – being able to deal with aerial balls will always be as important as being able to defend one on one.

Three versus three is fantastic for technical and tactical development but players will need to develop the more physical aspects of football. For this reason, we must use larger formats of play as well. Variety is important to player development so that they do not get stuck within a particular box. How the players' sessions are divided, and what weight is given to each, will dictate the attributes the players prioritise.

If this book were to be translated into a session structure it might look like this

1. Square based warm up
2. 1v1
3. 3v3 based practice
4. 6v6 (or larger numbers)

This is not hard and fast but more sessions would set up in this manner than any other style. When the session moves into the larger practices, we can still influence the way the game is played in accordance with our playing principles, and relate things back to what has been worked on in the previous segments. By choosing certain pitch 'types' (which we cover below), the game will play out in a particular way, without any coaching. The environment to continue practicing, yet having the freedom to create, can be dictated by appropriate pitch types. On a regulation pitch, it is likely that to achieve topic outcomes a coach will rely on heavy levels of intervention. This may work but players, in general, prefer a practice to flow. Individual interventions can keep the practice flowing but regular group interventions may result in an unhappy set of players, especially young players. The lines and shapes of the pitch create constraints for the practice; when these are linked with the topic, the outcome can occur more naturally without regular intervention. This means that when the coach does intervene, it carries greater value.

A clear use of lines to mark areas is in the creation of zones (and the once infamous zone 14; the area in which it was common for a number ten to operate).

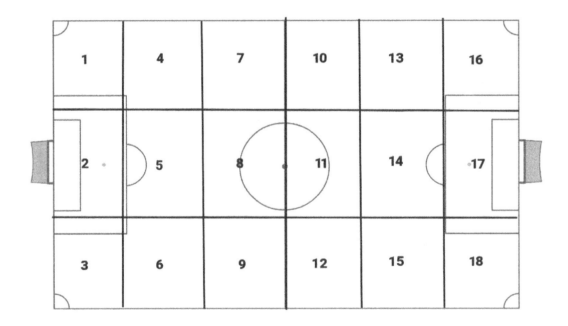

Pep Guardiola famously marks out his pitch into zones. Although these may not actually be physically drawn upon the pitch, the players are aware of them.

A basic version is simply a line through the centre of the pitch, running until the final third. Another line then runs across the top forming a T shape. The rules for this marking are that a left-sided player stays to the left of the centre line, and a right-sided player stays to the right of the centre line. This is until play enters the final third where players are free to move anywhere.

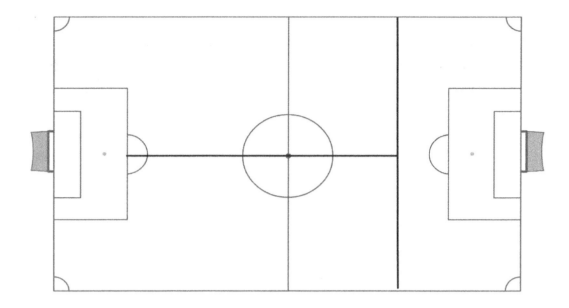

Guardiola's most famous version divides the pitch into multiple areas. His grid is comprised of 20 areas compared to the 17 more traditional zones.

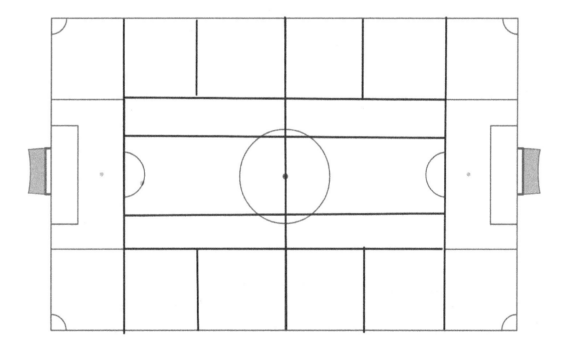

These zoned pitches are great examples of how a layout can be used to help players learn, and how the varying degrees of complexity can be an indication of the stages of learning of both the coach and the players.

1 – Regulation Football Pitch

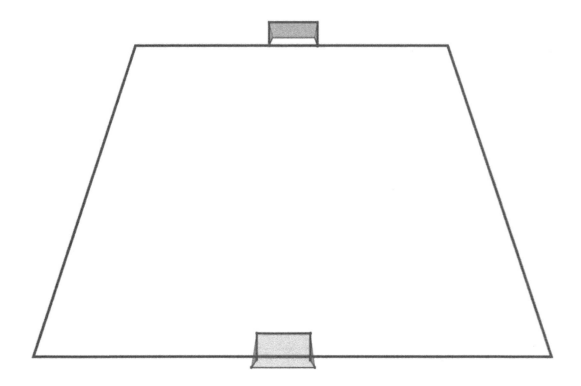

The pitch layout is simply that of the game in its most basic form. This simplicity makes the layout suitable for various conditions, such as one and two touch play, or finishing with one touch.

Coaches can also bring out any topic and outcome related to the game. However, the downside of this is lessening of freedom of decision-making for the players as their decisions are heavily coach-led.

Use for

- Anything

2 – Offset Goals

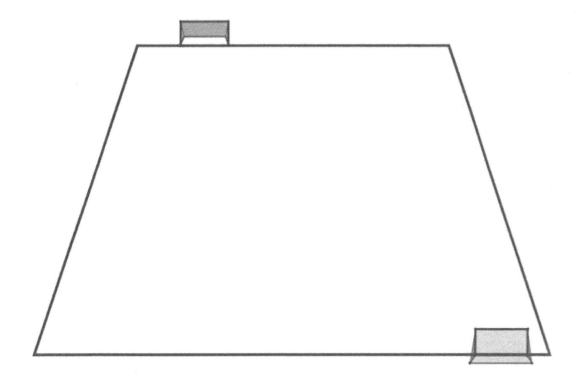

By placing the goals towards the corners of the pitch, the angles of the game and spaces to defend and attack are altered. When teams are defending the goal, they are likely to leave space in wide positions, which will create opportunities to cross or cut inside to shoot.

Use for

- Crosses
- Overlaps
- Cutting inside
- Defending crosses

3 – Four-Goal Game

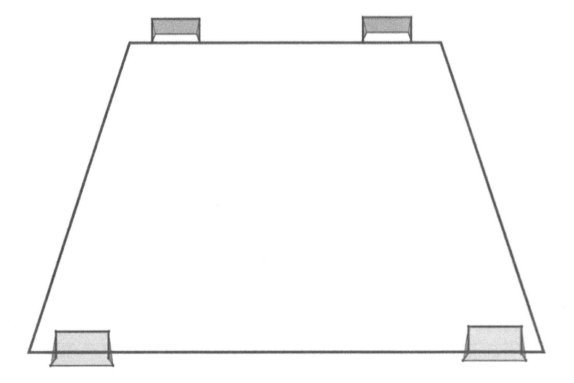

The four-goal game creates an environment where the players need to be spatially aware. This pitch works particularly well for groups where they don't use the width of the pitch or are clustered towards the centre. The lure of goals in wide positions encourages players to stay in wide areas away from the ball.

Use for

- Switching play
- Space recognition
- Movement

4 – Six-Goal Game

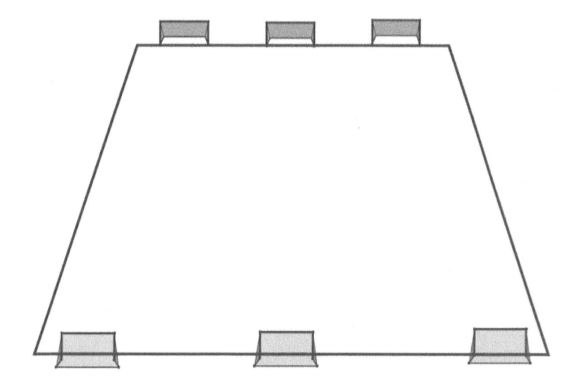

The six-goal game is an extension of the four-goal game. Increasing the number of goals on the pitch clearly increases the opportunities to score, making for a more exciting game with more options to create chances. The consequence of this is more finishing practice. It is also possible to involve a goalkeeper and set them the difficult – but not impossible – task of defending all three goals on their side of the pitch.

Use for

- Excitement
- Finishing
- Creativity

5 – Goals on All Sides

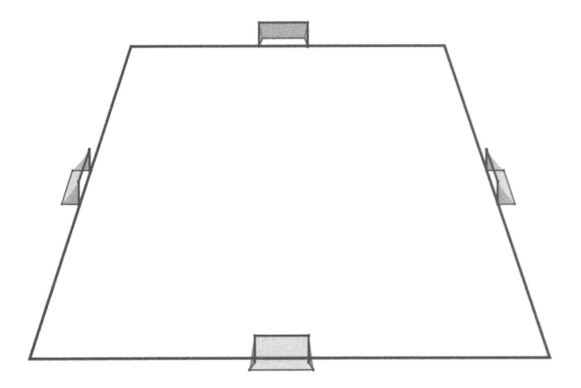

By placing goals around the pitch, the game is opened up through 360 degrees. Defending becomes very difficult but the array of attacking possibilities is increased. Using the same set up, we can have a number of situations:

- One team defending the two side goals (left and right), while the other defends the two end goals (top and bottom).

- One team defends the left-hand goal and the bottom goal, while the other defends the right-hand goal and the top goal.

- Both teams aim to score in every goal; the first team to score in every goal is the winner.

Use for

- Spatial awareness
- Goal scoring
- Creativity
- Movement

6 – Back to Back Goals

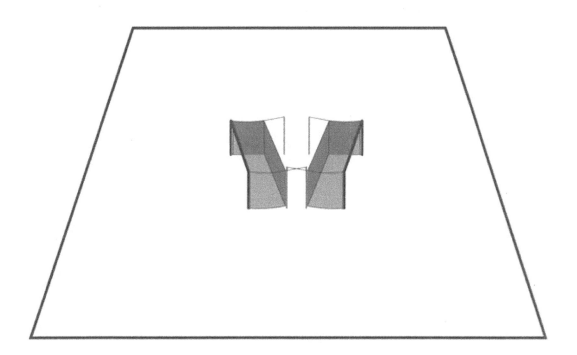

This setup gives players something different to think about. Players are able to occupy any area of the pitch, which encourages intelligent movement to find space. This, in turn, encourages players to look for intelligent and inventive passes. If goalscoring is too easy, an area around the goals can be added that players are not allowed to enter. Goalkeepers often enjoy this practice as they are kept busy.

Use for

- Spatial awareness
- Goal scoring
- Creativity
- Movement
- Positioning

7 – End Zones

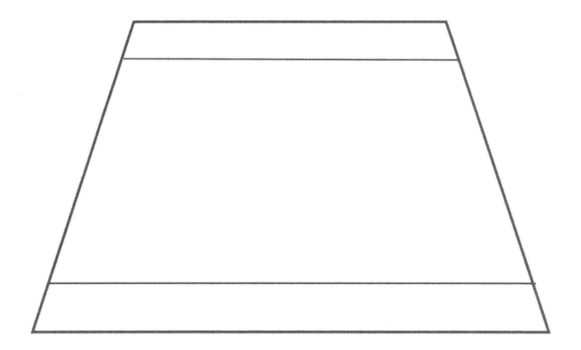

Using end zones encourages players to make forward runs with, and without, the ball. This also encourages passes that split defences.

The same setup can be used to position target players (one or two at each end) to create a possession-based practice.

Use for

- End zone
- Forward runs
- Dribbling
- Breaking lines
- Combinations

8 – Reversed Goals with End Zones

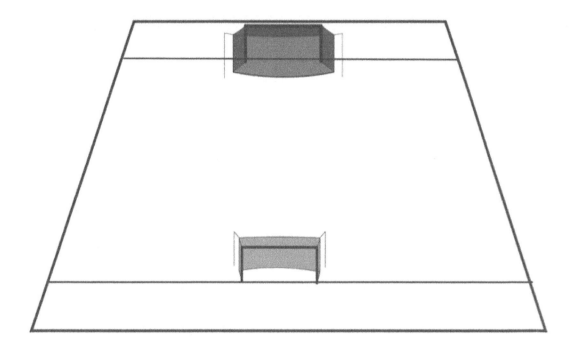

By reversing the goals, teams have to play into the areas before scoring. Teams can leave a player in the end zone to create a target. This player needs to have good movement to help create better passing options. The game combines elements of different setups which enable a variety of attacking combinations.

Use for

- Forward movement
- Man marking
- Overlaps
- Passing down the sides

9 – Horizontal Thirds

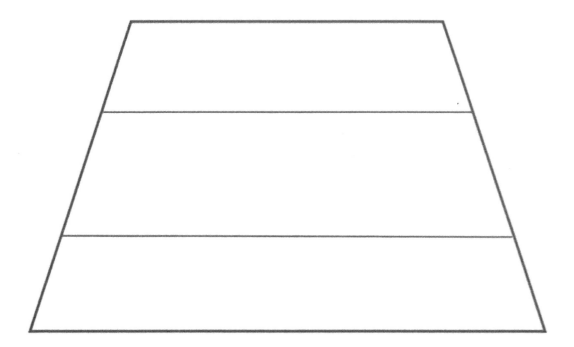

Dividing the pitch into three areas replicates the basic thirds of the pitch. This setup encourages buildup play using short passes. The game can end with a shot at goal (to be added in), or a point being scored when the end line is crossed.

If players are locked into their areas, it can make playing into the next zone difficult; but this can be a good tool for learning positioning. If players are locked in, but able to move into the next zone after passing forward, attacking movements come into play. Finally, allowing players to dribble into the next zone encourages the breaking of lines by dribbling.

Use for

- Through the thirds
- Playing out from the back
- Breaking lines
- Midfield build up
- Attacking overloads

10 – Magic Box

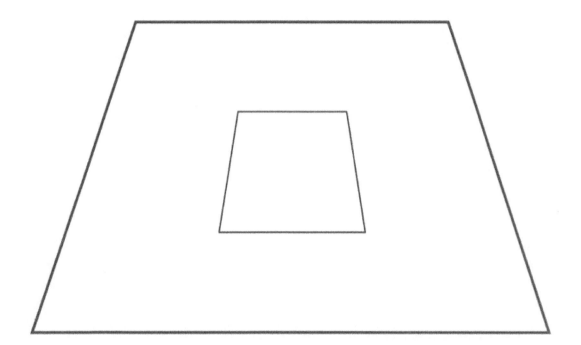

Using the box in the middle of the pitch encourages teams to penetrate the centre of the pitch. Players can move in and out of the box to create rotating movement in the middle of the pitch.

Defensively, teams can learn to defend the centre of the pitch and screen in front of the defence, preventing passes into areas that will hurt the team.

Use for

- Through the thirds
- Playing out from the back
- Breaking lines
- Midfield build up
- Overlaps
- Diagonal passes

11 – Vertical Thirds

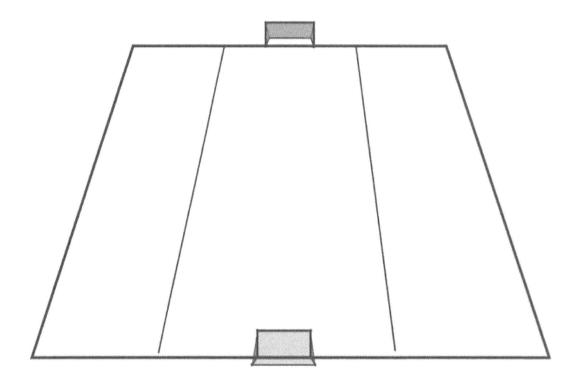

Similar to the horizontal thirds, but the focus here is on facing off with direct opponents, whilst maintaining width and shape. If we play with two players in each area, different types of combination play are applicable. Overlaps and underlaps from the wide positions. One-twos, set and spins, and crossover runs in the centre. Switching play and playing out principles also become applicable.

Use for

- Overlaps
- Width
- Rotation
- Crosses
- Switching play
- Defensive cover

12 – Corners

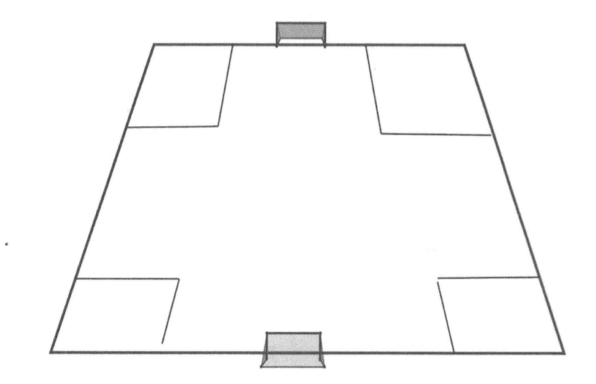

Players in corners can act as target players to play into before scoring goals. This will create crossing opportunities.

The corners can be left empty and players make runs into the corners, enabling work on combinations.

Conversely, the corners can be used as safe zones for defenders to receive the ball from the goalkeeper. This is pertinent to playing out from the back.

Use for

- Overlaps
- Crosses
- Targets
- Forward runs
- Playing out to full backs

13 – Central Area

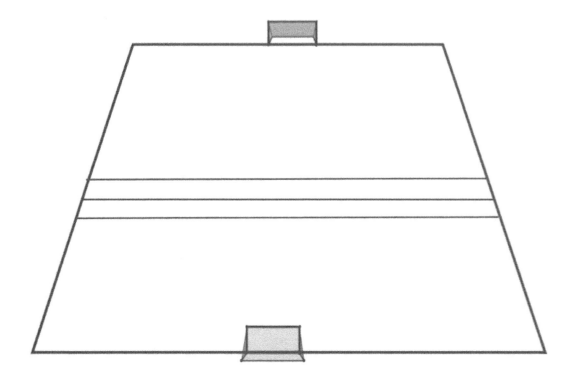

The two lines across the centre of the pitch create areas for midfielders to receive. Having two areas allows the players to pick up positions off each other. Having the rule that they cannot be in the same line, at the same time, encourages them to be offset and create angles.

The more advanced player of the two can receive and drive forward or move from the zone to join attacks. This will improve the understanding of one midfielder joining the attack and the other staying back to protect the defence. Should a team regularly play with three central midfielders, the area could have three lanes to replicate the positional play of three midfielders.

Use for

- Midfielders playing into forwards

- Turning

- Combinations

- Rotations

14 – Diamond Pitch

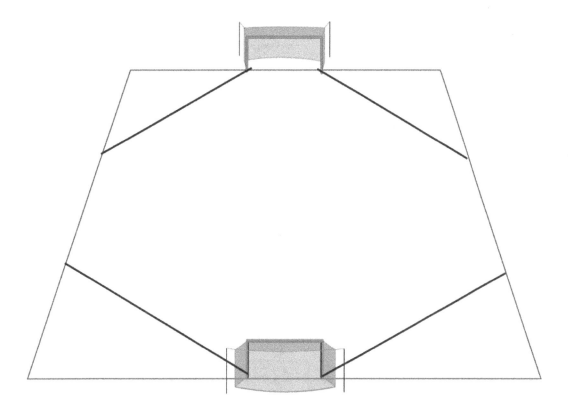

This pitch can be used in the same way as the pitch with corners, but can also be used for shooting and attack practices.

As the pitch tapers centrally, we can work on combination play in the centre of the pitch and players cutting in from wide positions to shoot. Adding a half way line can encourage shots from closer or longer range as desired.

The practice can also be used for central defenders as they will need to stay close to each other, developing their understanding of distances and their partnership.

Use for

- Cutting in
- Defenders and goalkeeper narrowing
- Angles
- Positioning
- Underlaps
- Combinations
- Forward runs

15 – Quartered Pitch

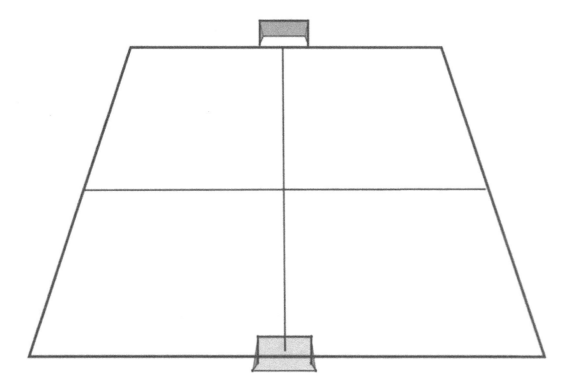

This pitch creates areas for players to occupy, in a similar manner to the pitches in thirds.

Depending on the numbers involved in the game, this practice will focus on 1v1 battles, overloads, or movement, in the quest to create and use overloads.

From a defensive perspective, this setup can enable players to develop an understanding of having a strong side and a weak side depending on the position of the ball (if the ball is on the left side, you want that to be your strong side; the right can be left exposed as the weak side because the ball is not there).

Use for

- Positioning/positional play
- Defending
- Support
- Combinations
- Movement
- Spacing

16 – Horizontal Quarters with Four Goals

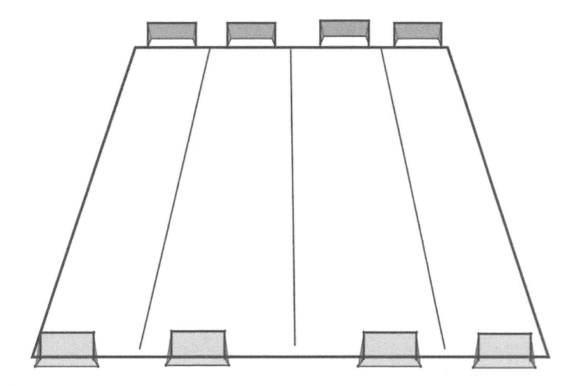

If players are locked into zones, we have 1v1 practices to work on.

Should the game involve four defenders with four zones and goals, the team that is defending has to be aware of a strong side, a weak side, and who puts pressure on the ball (and where). This is heightened even further if playing 3v3.

Offensively, four goals create lots of opportunities to score which will increase the creative moments available to players.

Use for

- Back four
- Screening
- Cover
- Attacking play
- Switching
- Creativity

17 – Circular Pitch

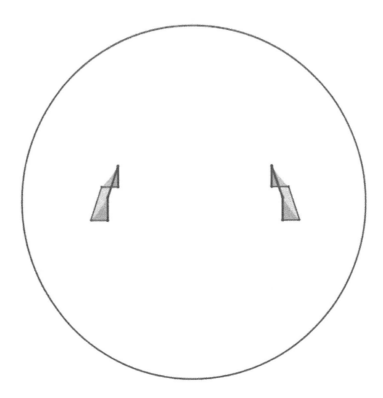

Using a circle creates a pitch that has spaces behind the goals. The lack of any corners will change the way that players use space and the way that they find it.

Use for

- Spatial awareness
- Movement
- Imagination
- Variations on other pitch types in 360 degrees.

18 – Wide Channels

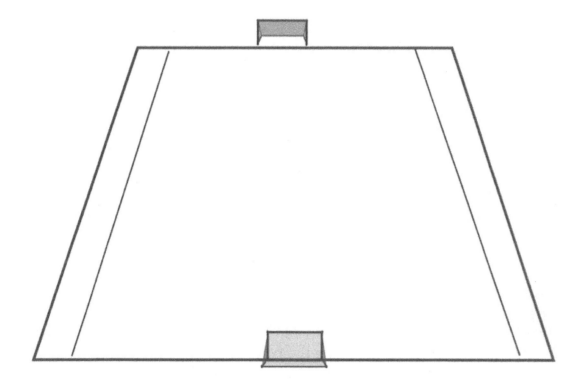

This pitch encourages wide play. The channels are usually safe zones containing support players. These players work their way up and down the line, helping the goalkeeper and defence to play out, making themselves available for passes that switch the play, and delivering crosses.

If the wide players are specific to teams, we can enable them to dribble on to the pitch when passed to. If the player who passes to them takes their place, we develop rotation in wide areas.

Use for

- Wide play
- Rotation
- Crossing
- Switching play

Concluding comment

It should be noted that these are not the only possible uses for these pitches; each pitch type can be adjusted by changing the type or number of goals used, or pitch shape. For example, pitch 18 could be combined with pitch 3 to change the focus of a practice.

7

A Practical Conclusion

Individual pieces eventually need to be pieced together. Once an element is fully formed, it melds together with others to create a whole. A team. Or a coaching session.

The simplest way to construct a session is by being linear. Increasing the levels of opposition and complexity until arriving at the most complex scenario of all: the match.

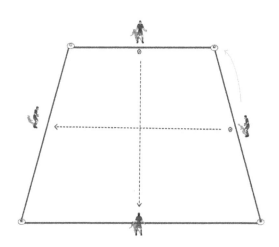

Warm Up Square

The players pass the ball across the square before moving to touch the cone. The players practise technique and timing.

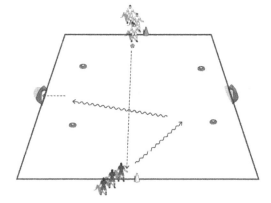

1v1

The players practise changing direction and accelerating away from the defender.

Chapter 7

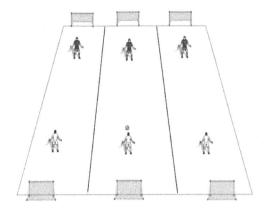

3v3

The players practise combining and beating their direct opponents.

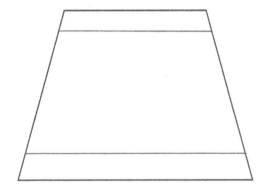

End zone game

In the end zone game, players score a point by either dribbling into the end zone or passing to a teammate arriving in the end zone.

Or

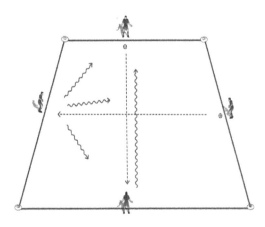

Warm Up Game

The receiving player attempts to dribble past the player who passed them the ball.

1v1

The receiving player protects the ball from the defender behind him before pushing away to the left or right and knocking the ball off the cone.

3v3 + Goalkeepers

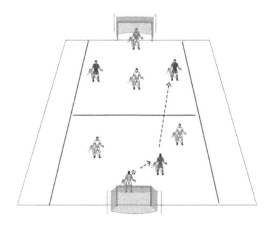

Two vs one in each half. Players look to combine quickly to score. The play starts with the goalkeeper each time.

Match

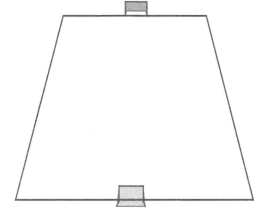

Straight game. Can the players use the elements from the previous practices to attack and score?

The choice of parts to train will depend upon your knowledge of your players and what they need, but the pattern does not always have to be this way. The gradual increase is logical but could become repetitive if adhered to for session upon session upon session.

The whole-part-whole session structure has risen in popularity in recent years. One of the reasons for this is that it provides what kids really want straightaway: a game.

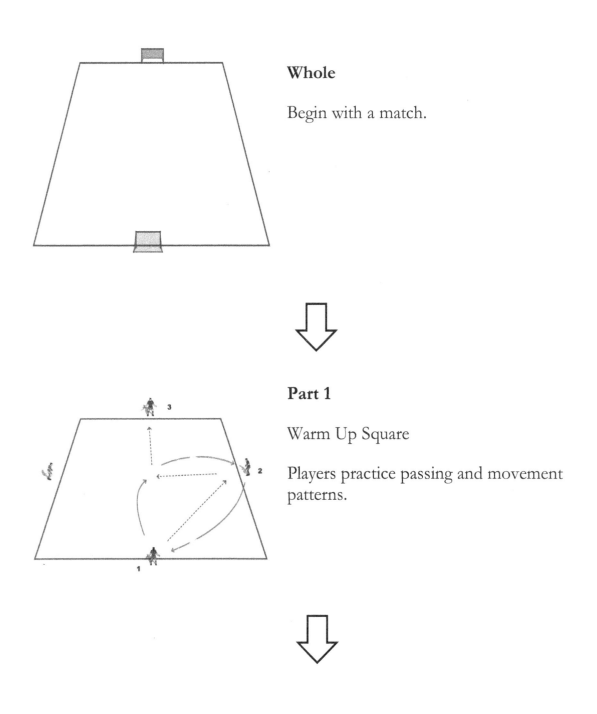

Whole

Begin with a match.

Part 1

Warm Up Square

Players practice passing and movement patterns.

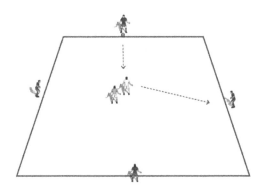

Part 2

1v1

Two players in the play 1v1 in the middle, using the outside players to help retain possession.

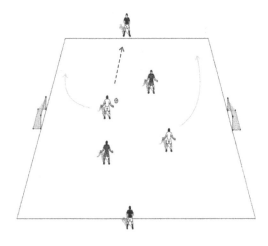

Part 3

3v3

The play is 2v2 in the middle. The white team uses the end players to retain possession. If the striped players win the ball, they score in either of the end goals.

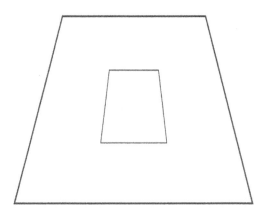

Whole

Magic square

The ball has to travel through the central square before the team can score by crossing the end line (goals can also be used).

Time depending, we might choose to skip past one or two of the parts. Our choice of which part to use (or which part to leave out) can be dictated by many factors. The age and level of the players; older players who may not need the pattern within part 1; younger players needing the pattern more than they need either part 2 or part 3, depending on their level.

The previous session might also help determine what is left out. If, in the previous session, patterns were worked on, then that might not be needed this session. Alternatively, the session might have been an opposed directional passing practice that the players struggled with, so the focus could be on the passing pattern and trying to incorporate that into a game situation.

Circuit-based structures can also be effective for tuning players into a session. If we believe the concentration and focus of our players begin to wane after relatively short periods, then we can move along at a pace that fits with them. There is an element of risk with this because a balance needs to be struck between concentration time and the time needed to grasp the practice. If players do not grasp the practice, they may not come out of it with the understanding they need. However, expecting players to master a topic within one session is unrealistic, so viewing each session as a part of a whole, or a set of linked practices, means players have the time they need to digest an idea.

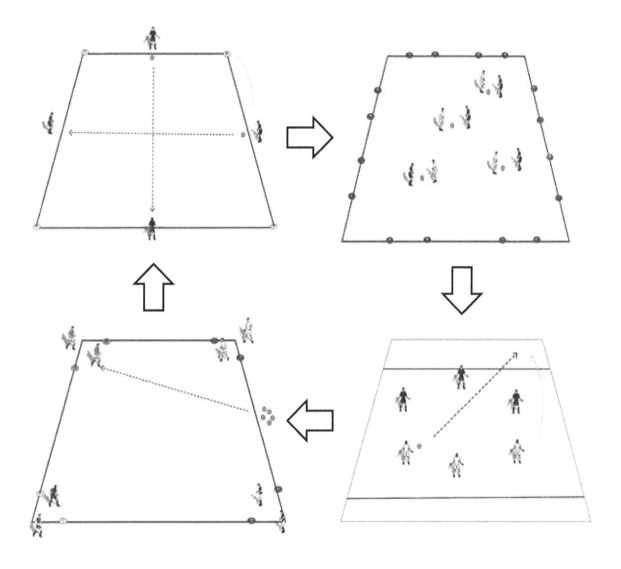

This circuit might then be followed by a larger-sided game that encourages dribbling and combination play.

Another possibility is to make such a set up competitive. With two teams of players spread across the areas. The players decide who plays in each area and the scores are added together. If multiple rounds are played, it should be possible to ensure players take part in each different game.

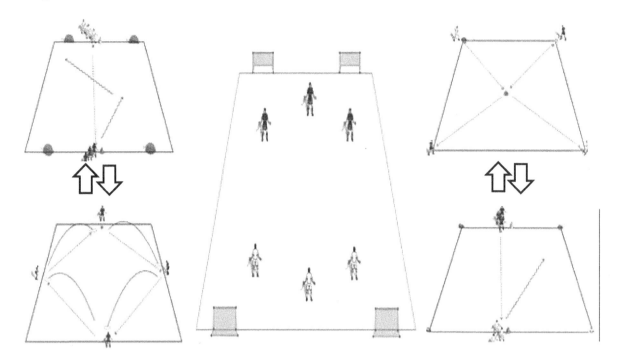

By being able to use circuit-based setups, we can cope with larger numbers of players at sessions and adapt, while still making the session engaging and exciting. Often, when coaches suddenly find themselves with far greater numbers than expected – targeted outcomes or topics are cast aside. By theming the areas, all players remain involved and specific areas of the game can still be the focus. In the above example, the overall theme in mind would be exploiting space on the weak side. The 1v1 practices look at dribbling towards the corners, the squares explore types of pass, and the four-goal game typically encourages players to stay wide.

A different choice could be to work on specific positions or with certain units. Without breaking into nuances, a team is split into three outfield units: defence, midfield, and attack. We can create a layout using 3v3 practices to work on these units.

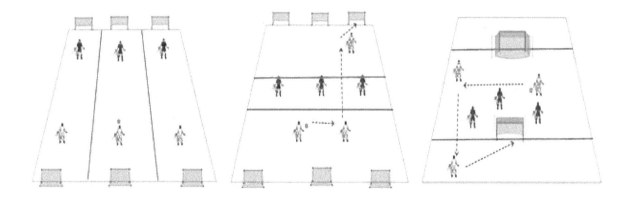

Area 1 focuses on 1v1 defending by locking players into their channels. The defenders have to make the choice whether to stay tight and defend man-to-man or be aware of the position of their opponent but stay away, defending their space as a priority. The set up also allows the defender closest to the ball to apply pressure and the two defenders away from the ball to take their positions accordingly. When the players are unlocked from their zones, there are additional aspects of the defence shifting across and the complication of tracking runners. (This practice might be used with a different focus at another time, looking at the combination play of the attacks.)

Area 2 focuses on both attacking and defending for central midfielders. Can the white team combine to play forward? Can the striped team stay compact and prevent a forward pass? If the stripes win the ball, they break out to score. The progression is for one stripe to come out and press, allowing two players to sweep up behind. A further progression is for two players to press and one to sweep behind. The time spent on each progression can depend on the system your team uses in midfield.

Area 3 has links to area 2 with teams attempting to play forward. The team in possession send a player into the end zone. They are a target man to play passes into. The goals are reversed so the forward needs to work on movement from side to side to create passing lanes. The forwards can be fixed inside the area. Another progression could be that the forward is not allowed to score but has to set the ball for a running teammate to finish. If the goalkeepers are working separately, they can eventually be joined into the practice. If they are not be being coached separately, they can be included from the beginning.

Setting up three areas in a row may also be useful in different environments where the monitoring of participants is important. Once again, this comes down to knowing the players and knowing who can be left to work independently and who needs extra attention to stay on task. Setting up multiple areas in a row allows the coach to patrol the space.

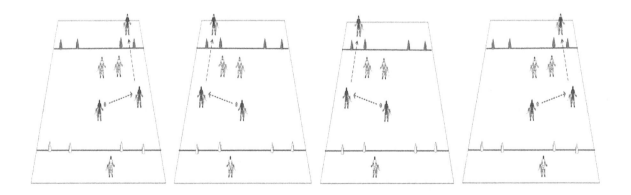

Setting the area up as square can also enable the coach to monitor all areas without moving. However, with some groups, this may not work as the coach will always have their back to someone.

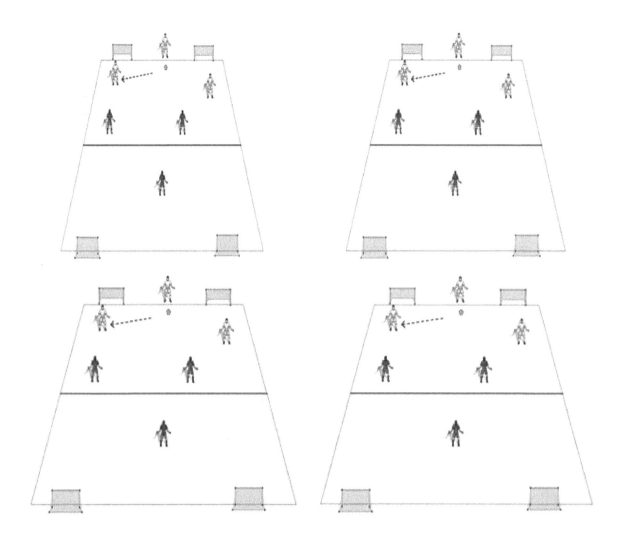

Coaching conundrums will always be around: time, outcomes, freedom, engagement and control.

- How can I best use the time?
- How can I get the outcomes for the players?
- How can I ensure the players have enough freedom to express themselves but stay on task?
- How can I ensure control of the group?

By using different setups, and well-designed practices, we can enhance our chances of successfully answering these questions.

A large part of the job of a coach is creating a positive environment. What does that actually mean, though? Players need to feel safe, not just physically safe but mentally and emotionally safe. Especially with young players. Safe to ask questions without being judged. Safe to be free. The knowledge that they are able to express for themselves is very powerful. The safety to make mistakes without being judged is vital to their development. 'Being judged' is the key phrase; mistakes will happen, mistakes will need to be acknowledged to help with improvement, but a mistake is not fatal and not something that will lead to a barracking. If we are to help players to reach heights of creativity, imagination, and invention, they must be allowed to fail. If they aren't failing, they aren't experimenting. In order for them to do so, they must feel safe.

Creativity is usually thrilling and exciting. Practices that encourage these things tend to be enjoyable. There has been a tendency to ensure that players have had a fun session. What do we mean by fun? Or enjoyable? What we really need is for a session or practice to be exciting. Exciting practices, overall, involve competition. A scoring system of some sort, or actual scoring. Goals make young players come alive; they make their hearts' sing. When they are practicing and playing, we need to ensure they have plenty of chances to sing. For them to be excited. Goals also have the added effect of making the practice directional, which adds extra realism. Good defending can be rewarded with goalscoring opportunities, and the encouragement of good defending. Launching an explosive counter-attack is far more exciting than kicking the ball out of play.

Therein lies the foundations of playing football. If, as a team or individual, we do not have the ball, it is highly likely that – at some stage – we will need to get it back. How we decide to get it back is a tactical choice that can be made on an individual, unit, or team basis. Once we have the ball, we then need to decide what to do with it. Do we attack at pace? Or do we retain possession of the ball? The match situation or even competition situation will dictate this. All of the elements of the game need to be experienced in order for players to reach their potential. Playing in triangles, recovering into position, switching play, dominating 1v1 situations – all of these technical and tactical elements will exist within the 3v3 setup. Players will have the opportunity to repeat the situations without repeating the practices. Players will learn match situations, while still being granted the safety to play with freedom.

Give the players excitement, and they will want more. The more they want, the more they will fall in love with football, playing for as long as they can and at as high a level as possible.

I hope that these practices can help them achieve that.

Other Coaching Books from Bennion Kearny

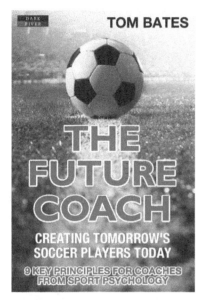

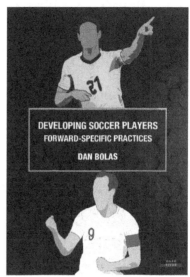

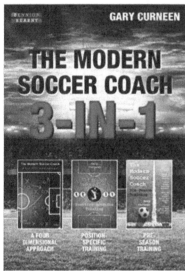

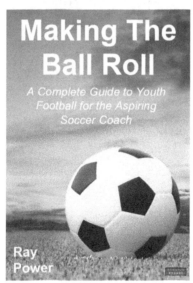

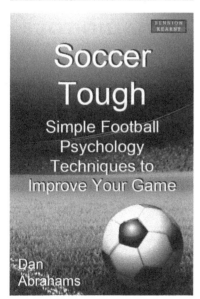

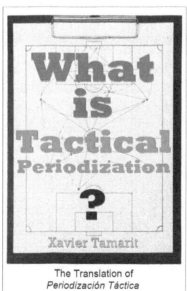

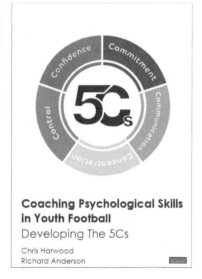

Other Coaching Books from Bennion Kearny

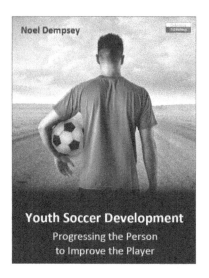

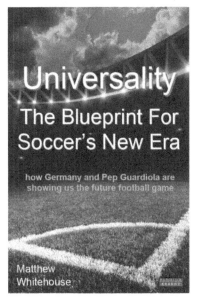

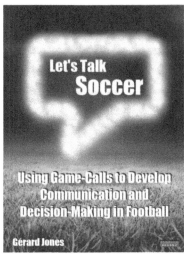

Printed in June 2021
by Rotomail Italia S.p.A., Vignate (MI) - Italy